# A New Owner's
## GUIDE TO
# OLD ENGLISH
# SHEEPDOGS

JG-146

**Overleaf:** Old English Sheepdogs photographed by Isabelle Francais

**Opposite Page:** Am. Can. Ch. Sniflik's Warwyck Forecaster, ROM, owned by Larry Stein and Linda Burns.

**The Publisher wishes to acknowledge the owners of the dogs in this book,** including: Linda Burns, Mrs. S. Keane, Marilyn Mayfield, Charles and Kathryn Schwarb, Dennis Snyder, Larry and Angela Stein, Henrik and Serena Von Rensselaer.

**Photographers:** Action Photography, Animal and Pet Photography, Paulette Braun, Warren Cook, Vicky Fox, Isabelle Francais, Gilbert Photo, Terrence A. Gili, Gillian Lisle, Robert Pearcy, Ritter Photo, Evelyn Shafer, Robert Smith, Missy Yuhl

The author acknowledges the contribution of Judy Iby to the following chapters: Health Care, Sport of Purebred Dogs, Identification and Finding the Lost Dog, Traveling with Your Dog, and Behavior and Canine Communication.

Distributed in the UNITED STATES to the Pet Trade by T.F.H. Publications, Inc., One T.F.H. Plaza, Neptune City, NJ 07753; on the Internet at www.tfh.com; in CANADA Rolf C. Hagen Inc., 3225 Sartelon St. Laurent-Montreal Quebec H4R 1E8; Pet Trade by H & L Pet Supplies Inc., 27 Kingston Crescent, Kitchener, Ontario N2B 2T6; in ENGLAND by T.F.H. Publications, PO Box 15, Waterlooville PO7 6BQ; in AUSTRALIA AND THE SOUTH PACIFIC by T.F.H. (Australia), Pty. Ltd., Box 149, Brookvale 2100 N.S.W., Australia; in NEW ZEALAND by Brooklands Aquarium Ltd. 5 McGiven Drive, New Plymouth, RD1 New Zealand; in SOUTH AFRICA, Rolf C. Hagen S.A. (PTY.) LTD. P.O. Box 201199, Durban North 4016, South Africa; in Japan by T.F.H. Publications. Published by T.F.H. Publications, Inc.
MANUFACTURED IN THE
UNITED STATES OF AMERICA
BY T.F.H. PUBLICATIONS, INC.

# A NEW OWNER'S GUIDE TO
# OLD ENGLISH SHEEPDOGS

## MARILYN MAYFIELD

# Contents

**1999 Edition**

6 · History and Origin of the Old English Sheepdog
Romans Classify the Breeds • Britain's Flock Guardians • Old English Not So "Old" • Tales of the Tail • The Old English in America

18 · Characteristics of the Old English Sheepdog
Case for the Purebred Dog • Character of the Old English Sheepdog

26 · Official Standard of the Old English Sheepdog

30 · Selecting the Right Old English Sheepdog for You
Health Concerns • Recognizing a Healthy Puppy • Male or Female? • Selecting a Show-Prospect Puppy • Puppy or Adult? • Important Papers • The Adolescent Old English Sheepdog

The Bobtail makes a wonderful companion and guardian of children.

The Old English Sheepdog is well known for his distinctive coat and cheerful personality.

52 · Caring for Your Old English Sheepdog
Feeding and Nutrition • Bathing and Grooming • Exercise • Socialization

68 · Housebreaking and Training Your Old English Sheepdog
Housebreaking • Basic Training • Training Classes • Versatility

A well-cared-for Bobtail will be a healthy loving companion.

138 · Identification and Finding the Lost Dog
Finding the Lost Dog

142 · Behavior and Canine Communication
Canine Behavior • Socializing and Training • Understanding the Dog's Language • Body Language • Fear • Aggression

88 · Sport of Purebred Dogs
Puppy Kindergarten • Conformation • Canine Good Citizen • Obedience • Tracking • Performance Tests • General Information

108 · Health Care
The First Checkup • The Physical Exam • Immunizations • Annual Visit • Intestinal Parasites • Other Internal Parasites • External Parasites • To Breed or Not To Breed • Medical Problems

The Old English is a high-energy dog that needs plenty of exercise and activity.

159 · Suggested Reading

160 · Index

A hardy working breed, the Bobtail has a long history as a herding dog.

124 · Dental Care for Your Dog's Life

130 · Traveling with Your Dog
Trips • Air Travel • Boarding Kennels

# HISTORY and Origin of the Old English Sheepdog

Regardless of breed, man's best friend, the dog, traces his origin to a common ancestor. Whether the breed is one of the purely decorative and diminutive Toy breeds or a member of the clever and hard working Herding breeds, a dog's ancestry eventually takes it back to none other than the one we know today as *Canis lupus*—the wolf.

The wolf's transition from creature of the forest to mankind's great friend and companion did not happen overnight. It began somewhere in the Mesolithic period over 10,000 years ago.

Man's chief occupation in those early days was simply staying out of harm's way and providing himself and his family with food. Considering the formidable obstacles that prevented him from doing so and his lack of tools when he wasn't fighting off predators, life was certainly no bed of roses.

There is little doubt that observation of the wolf could have taught man some effective hunting techniques to use himself, and many of the wolf's social habits might have seemed strikingly familiar. In turn, wolves saw a source of easily secured food in man's discards. The association grew from there.

As the relationship developed through the ages, certain descendants of these increasingly domesticated wolves could be advantageously selected to assist in hunting and other survival pursuits. The wolves that performed any function that lightened early human existence were cherished and allowed to breed, while those that were not helpful or whose temperament proved incompatible were driven away.

These wolves-cum-dogs were not only capable of deciding which game was most apt to be easy prey, they knew how to separate the chosen animal from the herd and also how to bring it to ground. These abilities did not escape the notice of man.

Richard and Alice Feinnes, authors of *The Natural History of Dogs*, classify most dogs as having descended from one of four major groups: the Dingo group, the Greyhound group, the

Mastiff group, and the Northern or Arctic group. Each of these groups traces back to separate and distinct branches of the wolf family.

The Dingo group traces its origin to the Asian wolf (*Canis lupus pallipes*). The Greyhound group also descends from a coursing–type relative of the Asian wolf.

The Mastiff group owes its primary heritage to mountain wolves like the Tibetan wolf (*Canis lupus chanco* or *laniger*). There is an odd assortment of breeds included in this group, ranging from the upland game dogs to bulldogs and mastiffs. This leads one to believe that this group is not entirely of pure blood. The specific breeds included have undoubtedly been influenced by descendants of the other three groups.

*The Old English Sheepdog's distinctive coat and enthusiastic personality makes him one of the most recognizable breeds in existence.*

The fourth classification is the Arctic or Nordic group of dogs, which is a direct descendent of

the rugged northern wolf (*Canis lupus*). Included in the many breeds of this group are the Arctic-type dogs, such as the Alaskan Malamute, the Terriers, and the Spitz-type dogs, including Schipperkes and Corgis. Also a part of this group are the true herding breeds. The Old English Sheepdog is one of the latter.

Almost all of the Northern group, like their undomesticated ancestors, maintained at least some of the characteristics that protect them from the harsh environment of the upper European countries. Weather-resistant coats were of the ideal texture to protect from rain and cold. There was a long coarse outercoat that shed snow and rain and a dense undercoat that insulated against sub-zero temperatures. These coats were especially abundant around the neck and chest, thereby offering double protection for the vital organs.

*Bred to serve man, the Old English Sheepdog has a long history as a tireless herding dog and faithful companion.*

Smaller ears were not as easily frostbitten or frozen as the large and pendulous ears of some of the other breeds. The muzzle had sufficient length to warm the frigid air before it reached the lungs. Leg length was sufficient to keep the chest and abdomen above the snow line.

This is not to indicate that there were no crossbreedings of the types or that abilities peculiar to one group may not have also have been possessed by another. In fact, some historians believe that many of the Northern dogs that retain a degree of hunting ability owe this strength to their Asian Dingo heritage, which is absent from other breeds whose ancestors were not exposed to this admixture. It is also believed that this cross provided some of these Northern breeds with a more refined attitude and tractability.

With the passing of time, humans realized they could manipulate breedings of these evolving wolves so that the resulting offspring became even more proficient in particular areas. While human populations developed a more sophisticated lifestyle, they also thought up new ways in which the domesticated wolves could be of assistance. Customizing the evolving wolves to suit growing human needs was the next step. They became hunting wolves, guard wolves, and herding wolves. The list of useful duties grew on.

*Over thousands of years, the Old English's natural instincts and abilities were selectively developed and they became the foremost herders and guardians of livestock.*

**ROMANS CLASSIFY THE BREEDS**
One can find documentation of controlled breeding practices by Roman writers as early as the first century AD. The Romans had actually broken down into six general classifications the various types of dog that was then referred to as *Canis familiaris*. These classes were similar to the "variety groups" used as a classification method by the American Kennel Club (AKC) today. Two thousand years ago, Roman writers talked of "house guardian dogs, shepherd dogs, sporting dogs, war dogs, scent dogs, and sight dogs."

Descriptions of the shepherd and herding dogs, which had undoubtedly descended from the Northern wolf, can be found in Roman writings as early as 36 BC. Granted, the dogs described were larger and fiercer than what is expected of the modern herding breeds, but in those early days the flock dogs were as much guardians as they were herders.

## BRITAIN'S FLOCK GUARDIANS

The Roman invasion of Britain introduced these flock guardians to the isles where they continued to protect the stock of the settlers as they had on the continent. The next wave of invaders to enter the British Isles emanated from Scandinavia. With them came another branch of the northern wolf descendants—the Spitz-type dogs. These dogs were typified by their Nordic characteristics—smaller in size than the Roman descendants and frequently distinguished by their black-with-white or sable-with-white markings and blue eye coloration. Some of the Scandinavian dogs brought with them the "chase instinct," which the island shepherds selectively developed into a herding and droving ability.

*The Old English Sheepdog's thick coat, bobbed tail and hardy build made the breed perfectly suited to withstand rugged terrain and harsh climates.*

Everything these Nordic spitz dogs brought with them suited the economic and climatic characteristics of the British Isles and blended well with the existing flock guardians. The smaller dogs were far less expensive to maintain and their more amiable temperaments made the dogs more trustworthy. Britain's cold, wet, and windy winter months were long and daylight hours short. The white marked dogs were easier to see when they were forced to work into the night. Even the "wall" or blue eyes were highly prized. It was thought then that dogs with this unique eye color would never grow blind, even at an advanced age.

## OLD ENGLISH NOT SO "OLD"

Old English as a language was spoken on through to the 12th century and our Sheepdog's name might lead one to believe that the breed's history dates back to that early time as well. However, the Old English Sheepdog or "Bobtail" as it is so frequently referred, might just as easily be called the New English Sheepdog. Until the 19th century, the terms English Sheepdog and Bobtail referred to any one of the many dogs used for herding livestock throughout the British Isles. The first dogs that might even be construed as resembling what is now known as the Old English Sheepdog did not come on the scene until the mid 1800s.

## TALES OF THE TAIL

Prior to that time, all the dogs used as herders or drovers throughout England were not surprisingly referred to as English Sheepdogs. As far as the Bobtail reference goes, it has far more to do with cutting or "bobbing" the tails of any of the abundant livestock dogs that were inclined to neglect their duties in favor of pursuing the wild game that existed in those days. While shepherds correctly believed that dogs used their tails as rudders, they also believed that docking the tails decreased maneuverability and discouraged the dogs from giving chase. The latter, of course, is probably closer related to old wives' tales than it is to reality.

Another reason for the docked tails was that the dogs used by the shepherds were "working dogs," not items of luxury like some of England's other breeds. As a result, the shepherd was exempt from paying taxes on the working dog. The stockmen therefore docked their dog's tails to indicate the tax-free status.

There is an erroneous belief that the word Bobtail implies that the breed is or should be born without tails. This is not true at all. An Old English Sheepdog born without a tail is not common and in fact is highly undesirable. It has been the authors' personal experience and has been agreed upon by many other breeders that Old English puppies born without a tail are not correct anatomically and usually have rectal abnormalities. The gene that creates this taillessness is an aberrant gene, yet this myth persists.

By the end of the 19th century, the Old English Sheepdog as we know it today was beginning to emerge. However, exactly what it took to shape the breed will undoubtedly remain a mystery. There is no doubt that England's herding and droving dogs figured importantly in the development of the breed. Some believe that the Bearded Collie from Scotland had his influence, and others credit the Russian Owtchar as part of the breed's ancestry.

At any rate, even into the late 1800s the breed was known as the "Short-tailed English Sheepdog" and relegated to compete at dog shows in classes with the far more popular Old English Sheepdogs. At that time, Old English Sheepdogs were called "Rough-coated Sheepdogs" or "Smooth-coated Sheepdogs" and exhibited accordingly. The Old English was, for all intents and purposes at that time, just another sheepdog throughout the British Isles.

*Ch. Lancelot of Barvan, shown here winning Best in Show at the famous Westminster Kennel Club show. Lancelot is only the second Old English Sheepdog to have this honor.*

## THE OLD ENGLISH IN AMERICA

The first Old English were registered with the American Kennel Club in 1885, but like in England, the dogs were only offered classes at shows as a variety of the much more popular Old English Sheepdog. From that obscure beginning, the breed began a climb toward recognition

that made the English take note and reconsider their lack of enthusiasm for the breed.

As American interest grew in the breed and prices began to elevate, it appeared that the English thought perhaps their shaggy friend from the pastures might have more to him than what had previously met the eye. History has proven that English breeders are entirely capable of breeding dogs to any make and shape they choose and that they can easily and readily customize a breed to a make and shape that has significant sales appeal. In England, the breed's appearance and quality improved in direct proportion to increased interest, and in time, many of the dogs found their way across the Atlantic to America's eastern seaboard.

One of the early importers was William Wade, a wealthy industrialist from Pennsylvania.

*The Old English Sheepdog rose quickly in popularity in the US throughout the 1950s. Henrik Van Rensselaer pictured with Ch. Fezziwig Artful Dodger.*

*Ch. Fezziwig Vice Versa was one of Hendrik and Serena Van Rensselaer's outstanding winners from their famous Fezziwig Kennels.*

Wade had become fascinated with the breed and had the wherewithal to support his interest. He imported a number of the dogs and hired Freeman Lloyd, the gentleman who had written the first official standard for the breed in England, to write a pamphlet extolling the many virtues of the unique breed. No stranger to the field of public relations, Wade distributed the booklets throughout New York, which at the time represented the sum and substance of the dog game in America.

J. Pierpont Morgan, another dog fancier and equally prominent and wealthy eastern seaboard denizen, became interested in the breed. Eastern society began to take note. In 1904, Wade and Morgan's Old English Sheepdogs were joined at Westminster Kennel Club by those belonging to the

Vanderbilts, the Dillinghams, and the Harding Davises, to mention only a few of the prominent names competing. The die was cast. The Old English Sheepdog had become a status symbol.

In 1904, the first championships were recorded for the breed and the Old English Sheepdog Club of America (OESCA) was organized. In 1905, the AKC officially recognized the group and although it has had periods of low activity, the OESCA has remained the parent club of the breed ever since, making it one of the 25 oldest breed clubs in America.

The breed remained property of the wealthy and influential on the East coast on through to the 1950s. In 1957, however, a litter was born sired by the English import and later American champion, Farleydene Bartholomew, which contained two puppies destined to become champions. One of them was to ignite interest in the breed from coast to coast and among people of all economic backgrounds. The litter was bred by Hendrik and Serena Van Rensselaer of Basking Ridge, New Jersey. The male was named Fezziwig Ceiling Zero and his sister was Fezziwig Black Eyed Susan.

Ceiling Zero, known as "Ceilie," shattered all standing show records and became a sire of great significance. The publicity he received with his many Group and Best in Show wins brought attention to a breed that had been literally unheard of among the general public. Ceilie's rollicking temperament, spectacular conformation, and striking markings and coat made the public at large think about having one of these marvelous "status symbols" for their own.

AKC registrations, which had barely reached 100 each year, began to rise rapidly. By the mid 1970s, registrations were averaging 15,000 a year. The symbol of affluence was finding its way into backyards and living rooms across America.

What the average dog owner did not stop to consider, however, was the amount of work involved in keeping the jolly family member clean and brushed. Whereas the wealthy were able to hire kennel help to tend to these chores, average Bobtail care providers realized they had

*Ch. Fezziwig Ceiling Zero's winning ways, outstanding temperament, and impressive show record did much to popularize the breed with the general public.*

acquired far more than they had bargained for.

Fortunately for the breed, this realization became known quickly, bringing annual registrations back down to a sensible number hovering around 2,000. By 1997, the AKC's registrations of just over 2,000 placed the Old English Sheepdog in a sensible 60th place among the 145 breeds registered.

# CHARACTERISTICS of the Old English Sheepdog

The Bobtail is first and foremost a total party animal—always happy and extremely intelligent. These characteristics work for and against the breed, because not everyone wants an overbearing, happy dog that not only wants but demands affection at an instant.

For years, obedience trial experts said that the Old English Sheepdog was not a good prospect for obedience training, implying that the breed lacked intelligence. Bobtail history totally contradicts this opinion. In order to be a good drover's dog, a breed must be both intelligent and dependable. What most obedience trainers fail to understand is that the Old English, like any good drover's dog, has his own agenda. Drovers are born with an understanding that there is work to be done and have the confidence and good sense about themselves to go ahead and get the job done.

*It is hard to resist an adorable Bobtail puppy, but make sure you have carefully considered the decision to bring one into your home.*

Trainers have the option of either frustrating themselves by trying to work against the Bobtail's inherent sense of purpose or take advantage of the characteristic and work with the dog. When training an Old English Sheepdog, one must recognize the fact that the breed loves to be the center of attention, so ignore unwanted behavior and praise desired behavior to the heavens.

Negative reinforcement tends not to work with an Old English Sheepdog. Even though it's negative attention, they still see it as attention. Anyone who is thinking about owning a

*The breed's protective instinct, high energy, and love of activity make them great companions for children.*

Bobtail must also be aware of the breed's herding instinct. The chase instinct is highly developed and they will herd a group of children playing as they would a flock of sheep. This can be extremely frightening to small children, particularly those who are not accustomed to large dogs. The positive side of this characteristic, however, is the breed's protective instinct. It is not at all unusual to see an Old English protect a child by placing himself between the child and a stranger.

Far too many prospective owners, impressed by pictures they see of an Old English Sheepdog or the jovial temperament of a friend's dog, will dash off to find a litter of puppies from which they can select their "baby haystack." Of course, what they find are adorable little youngsters ready to frolic.

Nearly all puppies are picture-postcard cuddly and cute and Old English Sheepdog puppies are certainly no exception. There is nothing more adorable than a litter of fluffy little puppies, nestled together sound asleep, one on top of the other. However, puppies are living, breathing, and very mischievous little creatures dependent upon their human owner for everything once they leave their mother and littermates. Furthermore, the fluffy and dependent Old English Sheepdog puppy quickly becomes a bundle of activity that has adolescent hormones that continuously rage and inspire relentless curiosity and activity.

Buying a dog, especially an Old English Sheepdog, before you're absolutely certain can be a serious mistake for anyone. The prospective dog owner must clearly understand the amount of time and work involved in owning any dog, especially one that requires extensive coat care and grooming. Failure to understand the extent of commitment that a dog ownership involves is one of the primary reasons why there are so many unwanted canines.

The Old English Sheepdog cannot be left to his own devices to live his life in the backyard. This breed wants to be in your face, so-to-speak. If someone is looking for a dog that requires minimal care and attention, the Bobtail is definitely not for them.

Before anyone contemplates purchasing a dog, some very important conditions must be considered. One of the first important questions that must be answered is whether or not the person who will ultimately be responsible for the dog's care and well-being actually wants a dog. If the prospective dog owner lives alone, all he or she needs to do is be sure that there is a strong desire to make the necessary commitment that dog ownership entails. In the case of family households, it is vital that the person who will ultimately be responsible for the dog's care really wants a dog.

In the average household, mothers are most often given the additional responsibility of caring for the family pets. Irrespective of the fact that mothers today are prevalent in the workplace, they are often saddled with the additional chores of feeding the dog and taking him to the veterinarian.

Pets are a wonderful method for teaching children responsibility, but it should be remembered that a child's enthusiasm might quickly wane. Old English coat care is a task beyond the average young child. You need to ask who will take care of the puppy once the novelty wears off.

Desire to own a dog aside, does the lifestyle of the family actually provide for responsible dog ownership? If the entire family is not home from early morning to late at night, who will take care of a young puppy? Feeding, exercise, outdoor access, and the like cannot be provided if no one is home.

Another important factor to consider is whether or not the breed of dog is suitable for the person or the family that he will be living with. Some breeds can handle the rough and tumble play of young children and some cannot. On the other hand, some dogs are so large and clumsy, especially as puppies, that they could easily and unintentionally injure an infant. There is also the matter of hair. A luxuriously coated dog is certainly beautiful to behold, but all that hair takes time to care for.

*In terms of grooming, the Old English Sheepdog is a high-maintenance dog. The time you want to spend on grooming should be considered before choosing a breed.*

Remember that the new dog must be taught every household rule immediately. Some dogs catch on more quickly than others and puppies are just as inclined to forget or disregard lessons as young human children.

## CASE FOR THE PUREBRED DOG

As previously mentioned, all puppies are cute, but not all puppies grow up to be particularly attractive adults. What is considered beautiful by one person is not necessarily seen as attractive by another. It is almost impossible to determine what a mixed-breed puppy will look like as an adult, nor will it be possible to determine if his temperament is suitable for the person or family that wishes to own him. If the puppy grows to be too big, overly hairy, or aggressive for the owner, what will happen to him then?

Size and temperament can vary to a degree, even within any purebred breed. Granted, there are all the acceptable variations within the Old English Sheepdog spectrum, but selective breeding over many generations has produced dogs that give the would-be owner a reasonable assurance of what the purebred Old English Sheepdog puppy will look and act like as an adult. The Old English Sheepdog is never going to be as lethargic as a Basset Hound, no matter where he may fall on the breed's temperament spectrum. Nor will an Old English Sheepdog ever be as small as a Chihuahua or as large as a Great Dane. However, there are certain facts. Expect your Old English Sheepdog to be nothing more and nothing less than what most other members of his breed look and act like.

A person who wants a canine companion for those morning jogs or long distance runs is not going to be particularly happy with a lethargic or short-legged breed. Nor is the fastidious housekeeper, whose picture of the ideal dog is one that lies quietly at the feet of his master and never sheds, going to be particularly happy with the shaggy dog that has a nose that is constantly pushing and prodding for attention.

Any dog, mixed breed or not, has the potential to be a loving companion. However, a purebred dog offers his owner reasonable

*The Old English Sheepdog's bobbed tail has earned him his nickname and contributes to his distinctive appearance.*

*Because he is a dog with a tremendous amount of energy and inherent sense of purpose, the Bobtail needs lots of attention, exercise, and training.*

insurance that he will not only suit the owner's lifestyle, but the person's aesthetic demands as well.

## WHO SHOULD OWN AN OLD ENGLISH SHEEPDOG?

Just as a prospective buyer should have a checklist to lead him or her to a responsible breeder, good breeders have a list of qualifications for the buyer.

1. The buyer must have a fenced yard or be willing to provide their Old English Sheepdog with the amount of on-leash exercise that he requires. We will not sell a dog to someone who wants to keep their dog in the backyard tied on a leash. This is an invitation for trouble.

2. The Old English Sheepdog owner must have time. This breed is not appropriate for anyone whose life is already completely filled with other responsibilities. It takes time to provide the necessary training, care, and human companionship that this breed requires.

2. The dog cannot be made to live exclusively outdoors with little human contact.

*Every member of the household must be willing to take on the responsibility of caring for your Old English Sheepdog.*

4. If the person buying the dog has children, we insist that the children come along. Children should be old enough and well supervised in order to be able to live with an Old English Sheepdog puppy's rambunctious attitude and the adult dog's 60 to 100 pounds of enthusiasm.

5. Everyone in the family must want an Old English Sheepdog. Both the husband and wife need to be interviewed to determine their desire to own the breed.

6. Many people are initially attracted to the Old English Sheepdog because of his impressive look, which is attributed to a huge amount of hair. This is not a "clean" breed. People

who come to look at a litter and are seen picking hairs off their clothes do not want an Old English Sheepdog, we assure you. If a sloppy mouth bothers prospective buyers, they are also not candidates for the breed.

7. We do not send puppies to their new homes on holidays, (i.e., Christmas) because it never works out. It is better to give the recipient a photo of the puppy in a card with delivery promised after the holidays. The stress of family gatherings and all the added activity is the worst time for a puppy to go to his new home.

8. All of our puppies sold as pets must be spayed or neutered and they automatically get restricted AKC registration certificates, which prohibits the dog from ever being bred.

*The Old English Sheepdog's most admirable characteristics are his devotion to and protection of the people he loves.*

## CHARACTER OF THE OLD ENGLISH SHEEPDOG

One of the Old English Sheepdog's most admirable traits is their devotion to the people they love. Although they don't have a hard or aggressive edge, the breed can be territorial. We personally know of an Old English that let a total stranger into the house with no problem. The catch was that the stranger couldn't leave. When the fellow tried to leave, the dog kept "herding" him into a corner and would not let him move. As mentioned earlier, if someone unknown or perceived to be a threat approaches a family member, the Bobtail will stand between the stranger and those he loves.

Someone who only wants a couch potato should look for another breed of dog. The Old English Sheepdog has been genetically gifted with intelligence, stamina, and endurance. To expect the breed not to use these characteristics is being terribly unfair to the dog.

# OFFICIAL Standard of the Old English Sheepdog

The standard of the Old English Sheepdogs is written in a simple and straightforward manner than can be read and understood by even the beginning fancier. However, it takes many years of experience and observation to fully grasp all of the standard's implications. Reading as much about the breed as possible helps a great deal but there is nothing as beneficial as putting yourself in the hands of a dedicated and experienced breeder if you sincerely wish to develop your knowledge of the breed.

**General Appearance**—A strong, compact, square, balanced dog. Taking him all around, he is profusely, *but not excessively coated*, thickset, muscular and able-bodied. These qualities, combined with his agility, fit him for the demanding tasks required of a shepherd's or drover's dog. Therefore, soundness is of the greatest importance. His bark is loud with a distinctive "pot-casse" ring in it.

*According to the standard, the Old English Sheepdog is a strong, compact dog that is muscular, agile, and able-bodied.*

**Size, Proportion, Substance**—Type, character and balance are of greater importance and are on no account to be sacrificed to size alone.

*Size*—Height (measured from top of withers to the ground), Dogs: 22 inches (55.8 cm) and upward. Bitches: 21 inches (53.3 cm) and upward.

*Proportion*—Length (measured from point of shoulder to point of ischium [tuberosity]) practically the same as the height. Absolutely free from legginess or weaselness.

*Substance*—Well muscled with plenty of bone.

**Head**—A most intelligent expression.

*Eyes*—Brown, blue or one of each. If brown, very dark is preferred. If blue, a pearl, china or wall-eye is considered typical. An amber or yellow eye is most objectionable.

*Ears*—Medium sized and carried flat to the side of the head.

*Skull*—Capacious and rather squarely formed giving plenty of room for brain power. The parts over the eyes (supra-orbital ridges) are well arched. The whole well covered with hair.

*Stop*—Well defined.

*Jaw*—Fairly long, strong, square and truncated. *Attention is particularly called to the above properties as a long, narrow head or snipy muzzle is a deformity.*

*Nose*—Always black, large and capacious.

*Teeth*—Strong, large and evenly placed. The bite is level or tight scissors.

**Neck, Topline, Body**—*Neck*—Fairly long and arched gracefully.

*Topline*—Stands lower at the withers than at the loin with no indication of softness or weakness. *Attention is particularly called to this topline as it is a distinguishing characteristic of the breed.*

*Body*—Rather short and very compact, broader at the rump than at the shoulders, ribs well sprung and brisket deep and capacious. Neither slab-sided nor barrel-chested. The loin is very stout and gently arched.

*Tail*—Docked close to the body, when not naturally bob tailed.

**Forequarters**—Shoulders well laid back and narrow at the points. The forelegs dead straight with plenty of bone. The measurements from the withers to the elbow and from the elbow to the ground are practically the same.

**Hindquarters**—Round and muscular with well let down hocks. When standing,

*An excellent example of the Herding Group, the Old English Sheepdog's overall substance and soundness make him fit for the demanding work of a shepherd or drover.*

HERDING GROUP

the metatarses are perpendicular to the ground when viewed from any angle.

**Feet**—Small and round, toes well arched, pads thick and hard, feet pointing straight ahead.

**Coat**—Profuse, but not so excessive as to give the impression of the dog being overly fat, and of a good hard texture; not straight, but shaggy and free from curl. *Quality and texture of coat to be considered above mere profuseness.* Softness or flatness of coat to be considered a fault. The undercoat is a waterproof pile when not removed by grooming or season. Ears coated moderately. The whole skull well covered with hair. The neck well coated with hair. The forelegs well coated all around. The hams densely coated with a thick, long jacket in excess of any other part. Neither the natural outline nor the natural texture of the coat may be changed by any artificial means except that the feet and rear may be trimmed for cleanliness.

*Ch. Trosambe Blue Panda St. Owly is groomed to perfection to show off the profuse double coat required of an Old English Sheepdog.*

**Color**—Any shade of gray, grizzle, blue or blue merle with or without white markings or in reverse. *Any shade of brown or fawn to be considered distinctly objectionable and not to be encouraged.*

**Gait**—When trotting, movement is free and powerful, seemingly effortless, with good reach and drive, and covering maximum ground with minimum steps. Very elastic at a gallop. May amble or pace at slower speeds.

**Temperament**—An adaptable, intelligent dog of even disposition, with no sign of aggression, shyness or nervousness.

***Approved February 10, 1990***
***Effective March 28, 1990***

# SELECTING the Right Old English Sheepdog for You

## WHAT TO LOOK FOR IN A BREEDER

Once the prospective Old English Sheepdog owner satisfactorily answers all the questions relating to responsible ownership, he or she will undoubtedly want to rush out and purchase a puppy immediately. Take care and do not act in haste. The purchase of any dog is an important step, because the well-cared-for dog will live with you for many years. In the case of an Old English Sheepdog, this could easily be anywhere from 10 to 15 years.

It is extremely important that your Bobtail is purchased from a breeder who has earned a reputation over the years for consistently producing dogs that are mentally and physically sound. Unfortunately, some people will exploit a breed for financial gain only, giving no thought to its health, welfare, or the homes in which the dogs will be living.

*To ensure against genetic disease and protect the quality of their programs, reputable breeders will screen all Old English Sheepdogs before breeding them.*

The only way a breeder can earn a reputation for quality is through a well-thought-out breeding program in which rigid selectivity is imposed. Selective breeding is aimed at maintaining the virtues of a breed and eliminating genetic weaknesses. This process is time consuming and costly. Therefore, responsible Old English Sheepdog breeders protect their investment by providing the utmost in prenatal care for their brood matrons and maximum care and nutrition for the resulting offspring. Once the puppies arrive, the knowledgeable breeder initiates a socialization process.

When the prospective buyer goes to look at a litter, the person should note how the breeder interacts with the puppies. The best puppies are born and raised in close proximity with their human family. They are imprinted with the scents and sounds of humans and even at their youngest ages, the puppies should be delighted to see the people that they have been brought up with. Puppies that are born in a

barn and given few opportunities to be with humans seldom achieve their full potential as companions. The buyer should look for cleanliness in both the dogs and the areas in which the dogs are kept. Cleanliness is the first clue that tells you how much the breeder cares about the dogs he or she owns.

The governing kennel clubs located in various countries around the world maintain lists of local breed clubs and breeders, which can lead a prospective dog buyer to responsible breeders of quality stock. If you're not sure of where to contact a respected breeder in your area, we strongly recommend contacting your local kennel club or the Old English Sheepdog Club of America for recommendations.

There is every possibility that a reputable breeder resides in your area who will not only be able to provide the right Old English Sheepdog for you, but who will often have both the parents of the puppy on the premises as well. This gives you an opportunity to see firsthand what kind of dogs are in the background of the puppy that you are considering.

Good breeders are not only willing to have you see their dogs but also to let you inspect the facility in which the dogs are raised. These breeders will also be able to discuss problems that exist in the breed with you and how they deal with these problems. As we have mentioned previously, do not be surprised if a concerned breeder asks many questions about you and the environment in which your Bobtail will be raised. Good breeders are just as concerned with the quality of the homes to which their dogs are going as you are in obtaining a sound and healthy dog.

Do not think a good Old English Sheepdog puppy can only come from a large kennel. On the contrary, many of today's best breeders raise dogs in their homes as a hobby. It is important, however, that you don't allow yourself to fall into the hands of an irresponsible backyard breeder, which is an individual who simply breeds dogs to sell. Backyard breeders separate themselves from the hobby breeder by their lack of responsibility. They do not use only dogs that have been rigidly selected to be free of genetic problems or health disorders. A hobby breeder's dogs find their way into the show and obedience ring or participate in the varied pursuits in which the breed excels.

If there aren't any local breeders in your area, check the Old English Sheepdog Club or national kennel club lists for reputable breeders. These established breeders are accustomed to shipping puppies safely to different states and countries.

Always check the breeders' references and do not hesitate to ask for documentation of their answers. The breeder will undoubtedly have as many questions for you as you will have for him or her. When you call a distant breeder, call at a reasonable hour and expect to have a lengthy conversation. The amount of money you invest in a satisfying telephone conversation may save you huge veterinary costs and a great deal of unhappiness.

## HEALTH CONCERNS

All breeds of dogs have genetic problems that must be paid close attention to. Even if a male and female do not have evidence of such problems it does not mean that their pedigrees are free of something that might be entirely incapacitating. Again, rely upon recommendations from national kennel clubs or local breed clubs when looking for a breeder.

*Before purchasing a Bobtail puppy, make sure you visit the breeder's facilities and that the puppies look clean, healthy and well taken care of.*

*Your Bobtail puppy will have a great start in life if his parents are healthy and well adjusted. Try to see the dam and sire of the puppy you are considering.*

Thoughtful breeders who are willing to breed selectively and discuss these issues openly can only eliminate breed health problems. It is important that you ask the breeder you are considering about hip dysplasia and juvenile cataracts.

Hip dysplasia is a degenerative deformity of the hip joint that causes lameness and in advanced cases, extreme pain.

Juvenile cataracts is an eye disorder with a premature onset of partial or total opacity of the part of the eye just behind the pupil. It gives the eye a milky or bluish look. The condition leads to a gradual or sometimes total loss of vision.

Nowadays, many breeders are also certifying elbow and thyroid function with the Orthopedic Foundation for Animals (OFA). Again, it is important that both the buyer and the seller ask questions. This is not to say that the puppy you buy or his relatives will be afflicted with any of the above, but concerned breeders are well aware of their presence in the breed.

*An Old English Sheepdog puppy should be a bouncy, happy extrovert that enjoys being around people.*

The gifted breeder uses all the answers you give to match the right puppy with the right home. Households with boisterous children generally need a puppy that differs from the one appropriate for a sedate, single adult. The time you spend in making the right selection ensures that you get the right Old English Sheepdog for your lifestyle.

If questions are not asked, then information is not received. We would be highly suspect of a person who is willing to sell you an Old English Sheepdog with no questions asked.

## RECOGNIZING A HEALTHY PUPPY

Most breeders do not release their puppies until they have been given their puppy shots. Normally, this is at about 10 to 12 weeks of age. At this age, the puppies are entirely weaned and can bond extremely well with their new owners. Nursing puppies receive temporary immunization from their mother. Once weaned, however, a puppy is highly susceptible to many infectious diseases that can be transmitted via the hands and clothing of people. Therefore, it behooves you to make sure that your puppy is fully inoculated before he leaves his home environment and to know when any additional inoculations should be given.

Above all, your Old English Sheepdog puppy should be a happy, bouncy extrovert. The puppies in a litter should all be very physical and playful with each other. The worst thing you could possibly do is buy a shy, shrinking-violet puppy or one that appears sick and listless simply because you feel sorry for him. Doing this will undoubtedly lead to heartache and difficulty, as well as costly veterinarian bills while restoring the puppy's health.

If the breeder permits, take the puppy you are interested in away from his littermates into another room or another part of the kennel. The smells will remain the same for the puppy, so he should still feel secure and maintain his outgoing personality. This will also give you an opportunity to inspect the puppy more closely. A healthy little Bobtail puppy feels solid and chunky, never bony or obese and bloated.

*Healthy puppies are a reflection of their breeder's good care. Every puppy in a litter should have clear eyes and a soft lustrous coat.*

The inside of the puppy's ears should be pink and clean. Dark discharge or a bad odor could indicate ear mites, which is a sure sign of poor maintenance. A healthy Old English Sheepdog puppy's breath smells sweet. The teeth are clean and white, and there should never be any malformation of the mouth or jaw. The puppy's eyes should be clear and bright. Eyes that appear runny and irritated indicate serious problems. There should be no sign of discharge from the nose, nor should it be crusted or runny. Coughing and diarrhea are danger signals, as are any eruptions on the skin. The coat should be soft and lustrous.

An Old English puppy should move about freely with no reluctance to use his legs. Of course, there is always a chubby,

*The more people your young Bobtail meets, the better adjusted he will be.*

clumsy puppy or two in a litter. Do not mistake this for unsoundness, but if you ever have any doubts, discuss them with the breeder.

## MALE OR FEMALE?

It is often thought that a spayed female makes the best possible pet in any breed. While this may be true of many breeds, it is not necessarily the case for the Old English Sheepdog; the sex is more a matter of preference on the part of the buyer.

Females do have their semiannual heat cycles once they have passed eight months of age. During these heat cycles that last approximately 21 days, the female must be confined to avoid soiling her surroundings with the bloody discharge that

*Although it's too early too evaluate this pup's show potential, Bobmar's April Luv knows she has that special something!*

accompanies estrus. She must also be carefully watched to prevent males from gaining access to her or she will become pregnant.

Teaching the male dog not to lift his leg to urinate indiscriminately to "mark" his territory can prove to be trying in some cases. However, most Bobtail owners do not find it difficult to correct their males in this respect.

Unless the dog has a highly developed herding instinct, Old English Sheepdog males seldom go wandering. They are far more interested in staying home to watch over their families.

It should be understood that most sexually related problems can be avoided by having the Old English Sheepdog altered. Spaying the female and neutering the male saves the pet owner all the headaches of sexually related problems without changing the character of the breed. If there is any change at all in the altered Old English Sheepdog, it is in making the dog an even more amiable companion. Above all, altering your pet precludes the possibility of his adding to the serious pet overpopulation problems that exists worldwide. It must be remembered that spaying and castration are not reversible procedures and once done, eliminate the possibility of ever breeding or showing your Old English Sheepdog in conformation shows. However, altered dogs can be shown in obedience, agility, and herding trials, as well as many other competitive events.

## SELECTING A SHOW-PROSPECT PUPPY

It should be understood that the most any breeder can offer is an opinion on the show potential of a particular puppy. The most promising eight-week-old puppy can grow up to be a mediocre adult. A breeder has no control over this.

Any predictions that breeders make about a puppy's future are based upon their experience with past litters that have produced winning show dogs. It is obvious that the more successful a breeder has been in producing winning Old English Sheepdogs over the years, the broader his or her base of comparison will be.

A puppy's potential as a show dog is determined by how closely he adheres to the demands of the standard of the breed. While most breeders concur that there is no such thing as "a sure thing" when it comes to predicting winners, they are also quick to agree that the older a puppy is, the better your chances are of making any predictions at all.

It makes little difference to the owner of a pet if their Old English Sheepdog is a bit too long in body or that the teeth might not meet in exactly the prescribed bite. Neither would it make a difference if a male pup has only one testicle. These faults do not interfere with an Old English Sheepdog becoming a healthy, loving companion. However, these flaws would keep that Bobtail from a winning show career.

While it certainly benefits the prospective buyer of a show-prospect puppy to be as familiar with the standard of the breed as possible, it is even more important for the buyer to put his or her self into the hands of a successful and respected breeder of winning Old English Sheepdogs. The experienced breeder knows that there are certain age-related shortcomings in young Old English Sheepdogs that maturity will take care of and other faults that completely eliminate the dog from consideration as a show prospect. Also, breeders are always looking for the right homes in which to place their show-prospect puppies and will be particularly helpful when they know you plan to show one of their dogs.

The important thing to remember when choosing your first show-prospect puppy is that cuteness may not be consistent with quality. An extroverted puppy in the litter might decide he belongs to you and if you are simply looking for a pet, that is the puppy for you. However, if you are genuinely interested in showing your Old English Sheepdog, you must keep your wits and without disregarding good temperament, give serious consideration as to what the standard says a show-type Old English Sheepdog must look like.

The complete standard of the breed is presented in of this book and there are also a number of other books and organizations that can assist the newcomer in learning more about the breed. Anyone wishing to breed or show dogs should fortify themselves with as much information as possible.

When I am selecting a show-quality puppy, all the foregoing regarding soundness and health apply here as well. I then look at the overall outline and structure along with the temperament. Markings are not relevant because our standard states "blue with or without white markings or in reverse." Many puppy mill owners and backyard breeders boast that all-white heads make a puppy better or more valuable. This is not true and is strictly a matter of personal taste. I personally prefer dark head markings, such as dark ears and/or an eye patch, but would never allow markings to influence my choice.

According to the AKC breed standard, when selecting a show-quality puppy, look for overall balance with no obvious faults. Even in an eight-week-old puppy, I expect to see easy movement. If we see a puppy struggling to pull himself up from a lying position, I would be very suspicious. All four legs should work together equally and easily. The right personality is also critical. I look for a puppy that has sparkle and charisma!

*Although all puppies will go through an awkward stage, your Old English Sheepdog pup should look a lot like his parents, only smaller.*

## PUPPY OR ADULT?

A young puppy is not your only option when contemplating the purchase of an Old English Sheepdog. In some cases, an adult dog or older puppy may just be the answer. One of the advantages of getting an older dog is the assurance of general good health. Up until about four to six months of age, almost anything can go wrong. If there are any major heart and liver disorders, they will usually start to manifest themselves between three to six months of age.

In breeds that are predisposed to hip dysplasia, the symptoms will usually become apparent before 12 months of age, and chances are that the dog will not develop obvious signs of the problem if they have not begun to show up before that time.

Getting an older dog also eliminates the trials and tribulations of housebreaking, chewing, and the myriad of other problems associated with a very young puppy. All this makes for a better job in determining compatibility.

A few adult Old English Sheepdogs may be set in their ways and while you may not have to contend with the

*If you do not have the time or the inclination to train a puppy, an adult Bobtail may be the perfect choice for you.*

problems of puppyhood, do realize that there is the occasional adult that may have developed habits that do not entirely suit you or your lifestyle. Arrange to bring an adult Bobtail into your home on a trial basis to find out if you are compatible with the dog.

## IMPORTANT PAPERS

The purchase of any purebred dog entitles you to three very important documents: a health record containing an inoculation list, a copy of the dog's pedigree, the registration certificate and health guarantee.

## Health Record

Most Old English Sheepdog breeders have initiated the necessary inoculation series for their puppies by the time they are eight weeks of age. These inoculations protect the puppies against hepatitis, leptospirosis, distemper, and canine parvovirus. In most cases, rabies inoculations are not given until a puppy is four months of age or older.

There is a set series of inoculations developed to combat these infectious diseases, and it is extremely important that you obtain a record of your puppy's shots and the dates they were administered. This way, the veterinarian you choose will be able to continue with the appropriate inoculation series as needed.

*Socialization with littermates will help your Old English Sheepdog get along with other dogs when he is older.*

## Pedigree

All purebred dogs have a pedigree, which is an outline of a dog's family tree. The breeder must supply you with a copy of this document authenticating your puppy's ancestors back to at least the third generation. The pedigree does not imply that a dog is of show quality. It is simply a chronological list of ancestors.

## Registration Certificate

The registration certificate is the canine world's birth certificate that is issued by a country's governing kennel club. When you transfer the ownership of your Old English Sheepdog from the breeder's name to your own name, the transaction is entered on this certificate and permanently recorded in the kennel club's computerized files. Keep all these documents in a safe place because you will need them when you visit your veterinarian or if you decide to breed or show your Bobtail.

## Health Guarantee

Any reputable breeder is more than willing to supply a written agreement that the sale of your Old English Sheepdog is contingent upon him passing a veterinarian's examination. Ideally, you will be able to arrange an appointment with your chosen veterinarian right after you have picked up your puppy from the breeder and before you take the puppy home. If this is not possible, you should not delay this procedure any longer than 24 hours from the time that you take your puppy home.

*Although your Bobtail puppy will be curious about the world around him, do not let him out to explore and make friends until he receives all his immunizations.*

Although reputable breeders get their breeding stock cleared for hip dysplasia and eye problems, it is important for people to understand that this does not give a 100 percent guarantee that the puppy will be problem free for his entire life. As breeders test each succeeding generation, it reduces the chances of problems cropping up, but there are never any guarantees that a 10- to 12-week-old puppy will stay problem–free for the rest of his life.

## Diet Sheet

Your Old English Sheepdog is the happy healthy puppy he is because the breeder has been carefully feeding and caring for him. Every breeder we know has his own particular way of doing this. Most breeders give the new owner a written record stating the amount and kind of food a puppy has been receiving. Follow these recommendations to the letter at least for the first month or two after the puppy comes to live with you.

The diet sheet should indicate the number of times a day your puppy was fed and the kind of vitamin supplementation, if any, that he was receiving. Following the prescribed

*The breeder should have started your Old English Sheepdog on the road to good nutrition, so be sure to follow this diet when you first get your puppy home.*

procedure will reduce the chances of upset stomach and loose stools. A breeder's diet sheet usually projects the increases and changes in food that will be necessary as your puppy grows from week to week. If the sheet does not include this information, ask the breeder for suggestions regarding increases and the eventual changeover to adult food.

In the unlikely event that you are not supplied with a diet sheet by the breeder, your veterinarian will be able to advise you in this respect. There are countless foods now being manufactured expressly to meet the nutritional needs of puppies and growing dogs. A trip down the pet aisle at your supermarket or pet supply store will prove just how many choices you have. Two important tips to remember are to read labels carefully for content and when you deal with established, reliable manufacturers, you are more likely to get what you pay for.

### TEMPERAMENT AND SOCIALIZATION

Temperament is both hereditary and learned. Poor treatment and lack of proper socialization can ruin inherited good temperament. An Old English Sheepdog puppy that has inherited a bad temperament is a poor risk as a companion, show dog, or working dog and should certainly never be bred. Therefore, it is critical that you obtain a happy puppy from a breeder who is determined to

*If you plan on working with your Bobtail in herding trials or in the field, be sure to socialize him with other animals. This shepherd gets an early start guarding his flock.*

*As long as they are properly introduced, a well-socialized puppy will get along with other pets.*

produce good temperaments and has taken all the necessary steps to provide proper early socialization.

Temperaments in the same litter can range from strong-willed and outgoing on the high end of the scale to reserved and retiring at the low end. A puppy that is so bold and strong-willed as to be foolhardy and uncontrollable could easily be a difficult adult that will need a very firm hand. This is hardly a dog for the owner who is very mild mannered or frail in physique. In every human-canine relationship, there must be a pack leader and a follower. In order to achieve his full potential, the Old English Sheepdog must have an owner who remains in charge at all times.

It is important to remember that a Bobtail puppy may be as happy as a clam living at home with you and your family, but if the socialization begun by the breeder is not continued, that sunny disposition will not extend outside your front door. From the day that your young puppy arrives, you must be committed

*Old English Sheepdogs make excellent playmates for children and caring for a dog helps to teach a child responsibility.*

to accompanying him upon an unending pilgrimage to meet and like all human beings and animals.

If you are fortunate enough to have children well past the toddler stage in the household or living nearby, your socialization task will be assisted considerably. Old English Sheepdogs raised with children seem to have a distinct advantage in socialization. The two seem to understand each other and in some way known only to the puppies and children themselves, they give each other the confidence to face the trying ordeal of growing up.

The children in your own household are not the only children your puppy should spend time with. It is a case of the more the merrier! Every child (and adult for that matter) that enters your household should be asked to pet your puppy.

Your puppy should go everywhere with you—the post office, the market, or the shopping mall. Little Bobtail puppies create a stir wherever they go and dog lovers will want to stop and pet the puppy. There is nothing better for a new puppy than affection.

*As an adolescent, your dog may question your authority. You must provide him with the proper training, guidance, and discipline he needs to succeed in all his endeavors.*

If your puppy backs away from a stranger, give the person a treat to offer your puppy. You must insist that your young puppy be amenable to the attention of all strangers—young and old, short and tall, and of all races. It is not up to your puppy to decide who he will or will not be friendly with. You are in charge and must call all the shots.

If your Bobtail has a show career in his future, other things in addition to being handled will have to be taught. All show dogs must learn to keep their mouths opened while a judge inspects their teeth. Males must be accustomed to having their testicles touched because the dog-show judge must determine that all male dogs are "complete," which means that there are two normal-sized testicles in the scrotum. These inspections must begin in puppyhood and continue on a regular basis.

All Old English Sheepdogs must learn to get along with other dogs as well as with humans. If you are fortunate enough to have a puppy preschool or dog training class nearby, attend with as much regularity as you possibly can. A young Bobtail that has been exposed regularly to other dogs from puppyhood will learn to accept other dogs and breeds much more readily than one that seldom sees strange dogs.

## THE ADOLESCENT OLD ENGLISH SHEEPDOG

You will find it amazing how quickly the little ball of fur you first brought home begins to develop into a full-grown Old English Sheepdog. Some lines shoot up to full size very rapidly, while others mature more slowly. A few Bobtails pass through adolescence quite gracefully, but at about seven to nine months of age most become lanky and ungainly, growing in and out of proportion from one day to the next.

Your Bobtail will attain his full height somewhere between 8 to 12 months of age. However, body and coat development continues past two years of age in some lines and up to three or four in others.

## Feeding

Food needs increase during this growth period and the average Old English Sheepdog seems as if he can never get enough to eat. However, there are some dogs that develop finicky eating habits and seem to eat enough only to keep from starving. Think of Bobtail puppies as individualistic as children and act accordingly.

The amount of food you give your Old English Sheepdog should be adjusted to how much he will readily consume at each meal. If the entire meal is eaten quickly, add a small amount to the next feeding and continue to do so as the need increases. This method will ensure that you are giving your puppy enough food, but you must also pay close attention to the dog's appearance and conditions because you do not want an Old English Sheepdog puppy to become overweight or obese. Excess weight on a breed that is prone to hip problems is extremely risky.

## Bloat

It is important that the prospective buyer is aware that the Old English Sheepdog is predisposed to bloat or gastric torsion. There is no known cause for it, but it is important that owners understand what bloat is and how to recognize the symptoms.

Bloat is a condition in which the stomach is distended with gas and twists in a clockwise direction until all internal organs are constricted. It is extremely serious and if not treated immediately can lead to the dog's death. Even those of us who are aware of the condition still lose dogs to bloat. If a dog is heaving with nothing coming up after having just eaten and his belly appears swollen, get him to the veterinarian immediately.

It is believed that free feeding or feeding your dog twice a day instead of one huge meal a day is helpful, especially with older dogs. Some breeders also suggest placing the food dish on a stool or box to elevate the dish up to a high enough level so that the dog doesn't have to lower his head all the way to the ground in order to eat.

*Large-chested breeds like the Old English Sheepdog can be prone to bloat. Feeding smaller, more frequent meals may help to avoid this life-threatening condition.*

At eight weeks of age, an Old English Sheepdog puppy is eating four meals a day. By the time he is six months old, the puppy can do well on two meals a day with perhaps a snack in the middle of the day. If your puppy does not eat the food offered, he is either not hungry or not well. Your dog will eat when he is hungry. If you suspect that the dog is not well, a trip to the veterinarian is in order.

The adolescent period is very important because this is when your Old English Sheepdog must learn all the household and social rules. Your patience and commitment during this time will not only produce a respected, well-behaved canine citizen, but will forge a bond between the two of you that will grow and ripen into a wonderful relationship.

# CARING for Your Old English Sheepdog

## FEEDING AND NUTRITION

The best way to make sure that your Old English Sheepdog puppy is obtaining the right amount and correct type of food for his age is to follow the diet sheet provided by the breeder. Do your best not to change the puppy's diet and you will be less apt to run into digestive problems and diarrhea, which is a serious condition in young puppies. Puppies with diarrhea can dehydrate very rapidly, causing severe problems and even death.

If it is necessary to change your puppy's diet for any reason, it should never be done abruptly. Begin by adding a tablespoon or two of the new food, gradually increasing the amount until the meal consists entirely of the new product. A rule of thumb is that you should be able to feel the ribs

*If you must change your Old English Sheepdog's food, do so gradually as to avoid stomach upsets.*

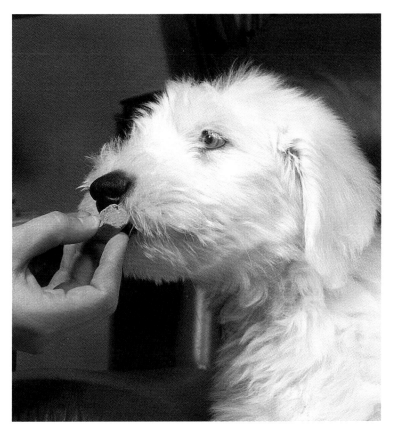

*Hard biscuits especially made for large dogs can become a highly anticipated treat for your Bobtail.* and backbone with just a slight layer of fat and muscle over them. It is important to remember that once a dog gets fat, he will not exercise and will be even more prone to weight gain. A vicious cycle begins, causing serious problems for heavy-bodied breeds like the Old English Sheepdog.

By the time your Bobtail puppy is six months of age, you can reduce feedings to two times a day, preferably in the morning or evening. It's important that you remember to feed your dog at the same time every day and that the food is nutritionally complete. By one year of age, you may wish to feed your dog only one meal per day, but I feel that two smaller meals are better for the dog's overall health.

A midday snack of hard dog biscuits made especially for large dogs can also be given. These biscuits not only become highly anticipated treats, but also are genuinely helpful in maintaining your Bobtail's healthy gums and teeth.

## Balanced Diets

In order for a canine diet to qualify as complete and balanced in the United States, it must meet the standards set by the Subcommittee on Canine Nutrition of the National Research Council of the National Academy of Sciences. Most commercial foods manufactured for dogs meet these standards and prove this by listing the ingredients in descending order with the main ingredient first on every package and can.

Fed with any regularity at all, refined sugars can cause your Old English Sheepdog to become obese and will definitely create tooth decay. Refined sugars are not a part of the canine natural food acquisition because canine teeth are not genetically disposed to handling these sugars. It's best to avoid sugar products, especially those that contain high degrees of sugar.

Fresh water and a properly prepared, balanced diet containing the essential nutrients is all that a healthy Old English Sheepdog needs to be offered. Dog foods come canned, dry, semi-moist, scientifically fortified, and all-natural. A visit to your local supermarket or pet store will prove the wide selection of dog foods that are available.

The important thing to remember is that all dogs, whether they are Old English Sheepdogs or Chihuahuas, are carnivorous (meat-eating) animals. While the vegetable content of your dog's diet should not be overlooked, a dog's physiology and anatomy are based upon carnivorous food acquisition. Animal protein and fats are absolutely essential to the well-being of your Old English Sheepdog; however, not all dry foods contain the amount of fat that will keep a healthy Bobtail in top condition.

This having been said, it should be realized that in the wild, carnivores eat the entire beast they capture and kill. The carnivore's kills consist almost entirely of herbivores (plant-eating) animals, and invariably the carnivore begins its meal with the contents of the herbivore's stomach. This provides the carbohydrates, minerals, and nutrients present in vegetables.

Through centuries of domestication, we have made our dogs entirely dependent upon us for their well-being. Therefore, we are entirely responsible for duplicating the food balance that the wild dog finds in nature. The domesticated dog's diet must include protein, carbohydrates, fats, roughage, and small amounts of essential minerals and vitamins.

Finding commercially prepared diets that contain all the necessary nutrients will not present a problem. It is important to understand that these commercially prepared foods do contain all the necessary nutrients your Bobtail needs. It is therefore unnecessary to add vitamin supplements to these diets in other than special circumstances determined by your veterinarian. These special periods in an Old English Sheepdog's life can include the time of rapid growth the breed experiences in puppyhood, the female's pregnancy, and the time during which she is nursing her

*Make sure your Old English Sheepdog has cool clean water available to him at all times.*

*There is no question that you will know when your Bobtail is hungry. This six-month-old pup lets his owners know it's chow time.* puppies. Even when required in these special circumstances, it is not a case of if a "little is good, more is better." Oversupplementation and forced growth are now looked upon by some breeders as major contributors to many skeletal abnormalities found in the purebred dogs of the day.

## Oversupplementation

A great deal of controversy exists today regarding orthopedic problems, such as hip dysplasia, which afflicts Old English Sheepdogs and many other breeds. Some claim these problems, as well as a wide variety of chronic skin conditions are entirely hereditary, but others feel that they can be exacerbated by diet and overuse of mineral and vitamin supplements for puppies.

In giving vitamin supplementation, one should never exceed the prescribed amount. Some breeders insist that all recommended dosages be halved before including them in a dog's diet because of the highly fortified commercial foods being fed. Still, other breeders feel no that supplementation should be given, believing a balanced diet that includes plenty of milk products and a small amount of bone meal to provide calcium is all that is necessary and beneficial.

*Your Old English Sheepdog should only be given supplements on the advice of your veterinarian.*

If the owner of an Old English Sheepdog normally eats healthy nutritious food, then there is no reason why their dog cannot be given table scraps. Table scraps, however, should be given only as part of the dog's meal and never from the table. A Bobtail that becomes accustomed to being hand fed from the table can become a real pest at mealtime. Also, dinner guests may find the pleading stare of your Bobtail less than appealing when dinner is being served.

Dogs do not care if food looks like a hot dog or a wedge of cheese. Truly nutritious dog foods are seldom manufactured to look like food that appeals to humans. Dogs only care about how food smells and tastes.

Most of the moist or canned foods that appear to be red, delicious meat only look that way because they contain great amounts of preservatives, sugars, and dyes. These additives are no better for your dog than they are for you.

## Special Diets

There are now several commercially prepared diets for dogs with special dietary needs. The overweight, underweight, or geriatric dog can have his nutritional needs met, as can puppies and growing dogs. The calorie content of these foods is adjusted accordingly. With the correct amount of the right foods and the proper amount of exercise, your Old English Sheepdog should stay in top shape. However, common sense must prevail. What pertains to humans also pertains to dogs. Increasing calories will increase weight; stepping up exercise and reducing calories will bring weight down.

*The Old English Sheepdog needs a tremendous amount of coat care and grooming to keep him looking and feeling his best.*

Occasionally, a young Bobtail going through the teething period will become a finicky eater. The concerned owner's first response is to tempt the dog by hand feeding special treats and foods that the problem eater prefers. This practice only serves to compound the problem. Once the dog learns to play the waiting game, he will turn up his nose at anything other than his favorite food, knowing full well that what he wants to eat will eventually arrive. Give your Bobtail the proper food you want him to eat. The dog may turn up his nose a day or two and refuse to eat anything, but you can rest assured that when your dog is hungry, he will eat.

Unlike humans, dogs have no suicidal tendencies. A healthy dog will not starve himself to death. He may not eat enough to keep himself in ideal shape, but he will definitely eat enough to maintain himself. If your Old English Sheepdog is not eating properly and appears to be too thin, it is probably best to consult your veterinarian.

## BATHING AND GROOMING

I might as well be totally honest about coat care. If not, someone that has never owned an Old English Sheepdog before is in for a shock. The tremendous amount of hair on his head easily attracts weeds, seeds, and mats that develop seemingly overnight. Unless your dog is kept clipped, you must plan on at least three to four hours per week for coat care.

The easiest way to groom an Old English Sheepdog is by placing him on a grooming table, which can be built or purchased at your local pet shop. Make sure that the table is at a good height whether you are sitting or standing. Adjustable-height grooming tables are available at most pet outlets.

Although you will buy the grooming table when your puppy first arrives, anticipate your dog's full-grown size when making your purchase and select or build a table that will accommodate a full-sized Old English Sheepdog.

## Grooming Equipment

You will need to invest in at least two brushes (three if you plan to maintain a show coat): a pin brush, which has long wire bristles set in rubber for the long hair; and a soft slicker brush, which has shorter, angled bristles to help break up mats that may occur. The third brush, and the best brush for keeping a full or show coat, is a natural bristle hair brush that is made for humans.

You will also need a coarse steel comb to remove any debris that collects in the longer furnishings, as well as nail clippers, a pair of good scissors for cutting hair, and a hemostat for removing hair that accumulates on the inside of the ear. Consider the fact that you will be using this equipment for many years and buy the best of these items that you can afford. Any attempt to groom your puppy on the floor may result with you spending a good part of your time chasing him around the room.

## Brushing

Teaching your Old English Sheepdog to lie on his side while on the grooming table can make your grooming chores infinitely much easier. Begin this training by picking the puppy up as you would a lamb, with his side against your chest and your arms wrapped around the puppy's body. Lay the puppy down on the table and release your arms, but keep your chest pressed lightly down on the puppy's side. Speak reassuringly to your puppy, stroking his head and rump. (This is also a good time to practice the stay command.) Do this a number of times before you attempt to do any grooming. Repeat this process until your puppy understands what he is supposed to do when you place him on the grooming table.

Start with the pin brush and edge of comb to begin what is called line brushing. Part the hair in a straight line from the tip of the nose, down the neck and shoulder, and straight on down to the rear. Brush through the hair to the right and left of the part, lightly spraying the area with water as you go. Start at the skin and brush out to the very end of the hair.

*Many breeds, like the Old English Sheepdog, need extensive grooming. There are kits available that provide all the equipment you'll need, including clippers, combs, brushes, and oil, to keep your dog looking neat and in great shape. Photo courtesy of Wahl Clipper Corp.*

Use the slicker only to get a loose mat out. A slicker is not an Old English Sheepdog's best friend unless you want a very thin and sparse-looking coat.

Do a small section—about a half inch—at a time and continue along the part. When you reach the end of the part, return to the top and make another part just to the right of the

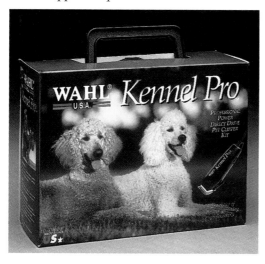

first line you brushed. Part, brush, and spray, repeating this process working toward the under belly.

I prefer to do the legs on the same side that we have been working on at this time. Use the same process, parting the hair at the top of the leg and working down. Do this all around the leg and be especially careful to attend to the hard-to-reach areas under the upper legs where they join the body. Mats occur in these areas very rapidly, especially during the time when the Old English is shedding his puppy coat.

If you encounter a mat that does not brush out easily, use your fingers and the steel comb to separate the hairs as much as possible. Do not cut or pull out the matted hair. Apply corn starch or one of the especially prepared grooming powders directly to the mat and brush completely from the skin out.

When you have finished the legs on the one side, turn the puppy over, and complete the entire process on the other side–part, spray, brush. With the puppy sitting, you can do the chest using the line brushing method, but it is just as easily done while the puppy is lying on his side.

Finally, check the hair of the "pants" on the rear legs to make sure that they are thoroughly brushed, especially around the area of the anus and genitalia. It is extremely important to be careful when brushing these sensitive and easily injured areas.

*If you can eliminate the tugging and tearing of your dog's coat in the detangling process, your dog will appreciate it and his coat is less likely to be split or torn. Photo courtesy of Wahl, USA.*

### Finishing Touches

When the line brushing process is completed, it is time for the finishing touches. Use your barber scissors to trim between the foot pads. Also trim the hair quite short around the anus. This will assist in keeping the area clean when the dog is eliminating. Thinning shears are also very useful in this area.

### Clipping

It has been my experience that mature and senior dogs should be clipped. Keeping the hair clipped to a short, tailored-looking length saves you hours of time and keeps your older fellow from having to endure endless grooming procedures. I clip everything but the ears. Clipping not only makes the dog's appearance more attractive, but it also helps the dog to feel good. Please understand that cutting off the hair over the eyes

*If you admire the fluffy, well groomed look of show dogs, you should consider using a hair dryer on your dog for after his bath. Start using it when he's a pup so he will learn to enjoy the experience. Photo courtesy of Metropolitan Vacuum Cleaner Co., Inc.*

will not cause the dog to go blind. This is only an old wives' tale that has no basis in truth.

Ear Care

The hanging ear of the Old English Sheepdog can create serious problems if it is not checked regularly. Because the ear flap covers the inside of the ear and blocks out air, that area must be kept clean and free of hair to avoid infection. The hemostat is used to remove the hair that grows there. Grasp a few hairs at the base with your hemostat and with a twisting motion, go slightly into the ear canal and remove them. Continue the process until all visible

hair is removed. When done in this manner, it should only take a few times.

When all hair is removed, swab the ear with a cotton swab that has been moistened with alcohol and thoroughly rung out. Never probe any further into the ear than the area that is visible to the eye.

Breeds that have hanging ears are also prone to hematomas (blood pockets) in the flaps. When they shake their heads, the blood vessels in the flap can break and leak, forming a pocket under the skin. Fortunately, this is rare in the Old English Sheepdog.

Apply a cold compress to prevent any further bleeding. This will also relieve any itching sensation that would make the dog shake his head even more so. Ice compress treatment alone can reduce and often eliminate the small hematomas, but large ones may have to be drained by your veterinarian.

## Nail Trimming

This is a good time to accustom your Old English to having his nails trimmed and feet inspected. Nail trimming should be attended to every four to six weeks. Your puppy may not particularly like this part of his toilette, but with patience and the passing of time, he will eventually resign himself to the fact that these manicures are a part of life. Nail trimming must be done with care because you don't want to cut into the quick. Dark nails make it difficult to see the quick, which grows close to the end of the nail and contains very sensitive nerve endings. If the nail is allowed to grow too long, it will be impossible to cut it back to a proper length without cutting into the quick. This causes severe pain to the dog and can also result in a great deal of bleeding that can be very difficult to stop.

The nails of an Old English Sheepdog that spends most of his time indoors or on grass when outdoors can grow long very quickly. Do not allow the nails to become overgrown and then expect to cut them back easily. If your Old English Sheepdog is getting plenty of exercise on cement or rough hard pavement, the nails may be sufficiently worn down. Otherwise, they must be carefully trimmed back.

*If you accustom your puppy to grooming procedures like nail trimming while he is young, he will soon enjoy the time you spend together.*

If the quick is nipped in the trimming process, there are many blood-clotting products available at pet shops that will almost immediately stem the flow of blood. It is wise to have one of these products on hand in case there is a nail trimming accident or the dog tears a nail on his own.

There are coarse metal files available at your pet emporium or hardware store that can be used in place of the nail clippers. This is a more gradual method of taking the nail back and one that is far less apt to injure the quick.

## The Wet Bath

If your Bobtail is well maintained and regularly brushed, frequent bathing will not be necessary, but there are occasions when a full bath may be required. On the occasion that your Old English Sheepdog requires a wet bath, you will need to gather the necessary equipment ahead of time. A rubber mat should be placed at the bottom of the tub to stop your dog from slipping and thereby becoming frightened. A rubber spray hose is absolutely necessary to remove all shampoo residue.

A small cotton ball placed inside each ear will stop water from running down into the dog's ear canal. Be very careful when washing around the eyes, because soaps and shampoos can be extremely irritating. A tiny dab of petroleum jelly or a drop of mineral oil in each eye will help prevent shampoo from irritating the eye.

Thoroughly wet your dog when giving him a bath. Do the head after shampoo has been applied to the body because very careful attention must be given to the head when soap and water are applied.  Rinse the head first. You must rinse the coat thoroughly and when you feel quite certain that all shampoo residue has been removed, rinse once more. Shampoo residue in the coat is sure to dry the hair and cause skin irritation.

As soon as you have completed the bath, use heavy towels to remove as much of the excess water as possible. Your Old English Sheepdog will undoubtedly assist you in the process by shaking a great deal of the water out of his coat.

Brush drying the coat with the assistance of a hair dryer (human or special canine blower) will significantly reduce drying time. When using a hair dryer of any kind, keep it on a medium setting. Anything warmer can dry out the coat and in extreme cases, actually burn the skin. Do not blow directly into the coat, but over it and use your brush to fluff out the hair and assist in the drying process.

## EXERCISE

As discussed previously, it is absolutely impossible to set hard and fast rules concerning the amount of exercise any Old English Sheepdog must have. Needless to say, puppies should never be forced to exercise. Normally, they are little dynamos of energy that keep themselves busy all day long.

Mature Old English Sheepdogs are not only capable but are delighted to be taken on long walks when the temperatures are not too high. Begin slowly and increase the distance very gradually over an extended period of time. Use special precautions in hot weather because high temperatures and forced exercise are a dangerous combination for the Old English.

*If the coat of your Old English Sheepdog is too much work for you to handle, you can always get him clipped. This Bobtail shows off his short and sassy look.*

Agility, flyball, obedience, and herding activities are wonderful exercises for your Old English Sheepdog's mind and body. There is no better way to ensure that your Old English Sheepdog has a happy, healthy existence.

## SOCIALIZATION

It should be understood that as stable as the Old English Sheepdog breed is, a young dog that has never been exposed to strangers, traffic noises, or boisterous children could become confused and frightened. It is important that a Bobtail owner give his or her dog the opportunity to experience all of these situations gradually.

# HOUSEBREAKING and Training Your Old English Sheepdog

Old English Sheepdogs generally are easy to housebreak. However, if the owner is inconsistent or lackadaisical in his or her approach, the Bobtail gets a mixed message and consequently, may do what he wishes.

Living through Bobtail adolescence is not unlike surviving the human teenage years—it does end and Old English Sheepdogs have a natural desire to please their owners. Adulthood will most often produce a dog that cooperates happily and joins in on any activity.

There is no breed of dog that cannot be trained; however, it does appear that some breeds are more difficult to get the desired response from than others are. In many cases, however, this has more to do with the trainer and his or her training methods than the dog's inability to learn. With the proper approach, any dog that is not mentally deficient can be taught to be a good canine citizen. Many dog owners do not understand how a dog learns, nor do they realize that they can be breed specific in their approach to training.

*With the proper motivation and guidance, the intelligent Old English Sheepdog can be easily housebroken.*

Young Bobtail puppies have an amazing capacity to learn that is greater than most humans realize. However, it is important to remember that these young puppies also quickly forget unless they are reminded of what they have learned by continual reinforcement.

As Bobtail puppies leave the nest they begin their search for two things: a pack leader and the rules set down by that

*Just like babies, puppies have very short attention spans. However, with persistence, praise, and repetition, your Bobtail will learn what you want to teach him.*

leader by which the puppies can abide. Too many owners fail miserably in supplying these very basic needs. Instead, the owner immediately begins to respond to the demands of the puppy, and Bobtail puppies can be very demanding.

For example, a Bobtail puppy quickly learns that he will be allowed into the house because he is whining and not because he can only enter the house when he is not whining. Instead of learning that the only way he will be fed is to follow a set procedure (i.e., sitting or lying down on command) the poorly educated Bobtail puppy learns that leaping about the kitchen and creating a stir is what gets results.

If the young Bobtail puppy cannot find his pack leader in an owner, he will rapidly assume the role of pack leader. If there are no rules imposed, the puppy learns to make his own rules.

Unfortunately, the negligent owner continually reinforces the puppy's decisions by allowing him to govern the household. The key to successful training lies in establishing the proper relationship between dog and owner. The owner or the owning family must designate their role as pack leader and immediately establish house rules.

The Old English Sheepdog is easily trained to do almost any task. It is important to remember, however, that the breed does not comprehend violent treatment, *Crate training is the fastest and easiest method to housebreak your Old English Sheepdog.* nor does the Bobtail need it. Positive reinforcement is the key to training an Old English Sheepdog successfully. Always show your dog the right thing to do and be consistent with your commands.

## HOUSEBREAKING

The most successful method of housebreaking is to avoid accidents from happening in the first place. We take a puppy outdoors to relieve himself after every meal, after every nap, and after every 15 or 20 minutes of playtime. Carry the puppy outdoors to avoid the opportunity of an accident occurring on the way.

Housebreaking your Old English Sheepdog becomes a much easier task with the use of a crate. Most breeders use the extra large fiberglass-type crates approved by the airlines for shipping live animals. They are easy to clean and can be used for the dog's entire life. Some first-time dog owners may see the crate method as cruel, but what they do not understand is that all dogs need a place of their own to retreat. A puppy will soon look to his crate as his own private den.

Using a crate reduces housetraining time to an absolute minimum and avoids keeping a puppy under constant stress by incessantly correcting him for making mistakes in the house. The anti-crate advocates who consider it cruel to confine a puppy for any length of time do not seem to have a problem with constantly harassing and punishing the puppy because he wet on the carpet and relieved himself behind the sofa.

Begin feeding your Bobtail puppy in the crate, keeping the door closed and latched while the puppy is eating. When the meal is finished, open the cage and carry the puppy outdoors

*Your Bobtail will soon come to think of his crate as a cozy den in which to retreat and relax.*

to the spot where you want him to eliminate. In the event that you do not have outdoor access or will be away from home for long periods of time, begin housebreaking by placing newspapers in some out of the way corner that is easily accessible to the puppy. If you consistently take your puppy to the same spot, you will reinforce the habit of going there for that purpose.

It is important that you do not let the puppy loose after eating because young puppies will eliminate almost immediately after eating or drinking. They will also be ready to relieve themselves when they first wake up and after playing. If you keep a watchful eye on your puppy you will quickly learn when this is about to take place. A puppy usually circles and sniffs the floor just before he will relieve itself. Do not give your puppy an opportunity to learn that he can eliminate in the house! Your housetraining chores will be reduced considerably if you avoid bad habits from forming in the first place.

If you are not able to watch your puppy every minute, he should be in his crate with the door securely latched. Each time you put your puppy in the crate, give him a small treat of some kind. Throw the treat to the back of the cage and encourage the puppy to walk in on his own. When he does so, praise the puppy and perhaps hand him another piece of the treat through the wires of the cage.

*Puppies have to eliminate after eating, drinking, sleeping, and playing. If you take your puppy to the same place outside each time, he will soon know what is expected of him.*

Do understand that an Old English Sheepdog puppy of eight to twelve weeks will not be able to contain himself for long periods of time. Puppies of that age must relieve themselves often except at night, so adjust your schedule accordingly. Also, make sure that your puppy has relieved himself at night before the last member of the family retires.

Your first priority in the morning is to get the puppy outdoors. Just how early this will take place will depend much more on your puppy than on you. If your Bobtail is like most others, there will be no doubt in your mind when he needs to be let out. You will also very quickly learn how to tell the difference between the puppy's emergency signals and just unhappy grumbling. Do not test the young puppy's ability to contain himself. His vocal demand to be let out is confirmation that the housebreaking lesson is being learned.

If you have to be away from home all day, you can't leave your puppy in a crate; however, do not make the mistake of allowing him to roam the house. Confine the puppy to a small room or partitioned-off area and cover the floor with newspaper. Make this area large enough so that the puppy will not have to relieve himself next to his bed, food, or water bowls. You will soon find that the puppy will be inclined to use one particular spot to perform his bowel and bladder functions. When you are home, you must take the puppy to this exact spot to eliminate at the appropriate time.

*Old English Sheepdogs can excel in obedience training. Ch. Sniflik's Warwyck Forecaster was the youngest owner-handled of his breed to finish his championship.*

## BASIC TRAINING

Training should never take place when you are irritated, distressed, or preoccupied. Nor should you begin basic training in crowded or noisy places that will interfere with you or your dog's

*It may take some time for your puppy to get used to his collar and leash, but soon he will not even remember he is wearing it.*

concentration. Once the commands are understood and learned you can begin testing your dog in public places, but at first, the two of you should work in a place where you can concentrate fully upon each other.

## The No Command

There is no doubt that one of the most important commands your Bobtail puppy will ever learn is the no command. It is extremely important that your puppy learns this command as soon as possible. One important piece of advice in using this and all other commands is to never give an Old English Sheepdog a command that you are not prepared and able to enforce. The only way a puppy learns to obey commands is to realize that once issued, commands must be complied with. Learning the no command should start the first day of the puppy's arrival at your home.

## Leash Training

It is never too early to accustom your Bobtail puppy to his leash and collar. The leash and collar is your fail-safe way of keeping your dog under control. It may not be necessary for the puppy or adult Bobtail to wear his collar and identification tags within the confines of your home, but no dog should ever be outside without a collar and leash.

It is best to begin to get your puppy accustomed to his collar by leaving it around his neck for a few minutes at a time, gradually increasing the time that you leave the collar on. Most Bobtail puppies become accustomed to their collar very quickly and after a few scratches to remove it, forget they are even wearing one.

*Retractable leashes provide dogs with freedom while allowing the owner complete control. Leashes are available in a wide variety of lengths for all breeds of dog. Photo courtesy of Flexi-USA, Inc.*

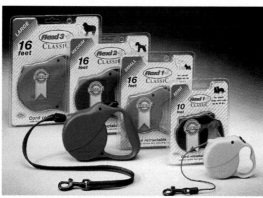

While you are playing with the puppy, attach a lightweight leash to the collar. Do not try to guide the puppy at first. The point here is to accustom the puppy to the feeling of having something attached to the collar. Encourage your puppy to follow you as you move away. If the puppy is reluctant to cooperate, coax him along with a treat of some kind. Hold the treat in front of the puppy's nose to encourage him to follow you. Just as soon as the puppy takes a few steps toward you, praise him enthusiastically and continue to do so as you continue to move along.

Make the initial sessions short and fun and continue the lessons in your home or yard until the puppy is completely unconcerned about the fact that he is on a leash. With a treat in one hand and the leash in the other, you can use both to guide the puppy in the direction that you wish to go. Begin your first walks in front of the house, extending them down the street and eventually around the block.

*Once your Old English Sheepdog is able to walk nicely on his leash, you can enjoy going out and about together.*

## The Come Command

The next most important lesson for the Old English Sheepdog puppy to learn is to come when called. Therefore, it is very important that the puppy learn his name as soon as possible. Constantly repeating the dog's name is what does the trick. Use the puppy's name every time you speak to him. For example, "Want to go outside, Buster?" "Come Buster, come!"

Learning to come on command could save your Old English Sheepdog's life when the two of you venture out into the world. Although the come command has to be obeyed without question, the dog should not associate it with fear. Your dog's response to his name and the word come should always be associated with a pleasant experience, such as receiving praise or a food treat.

All too often, novice trainers get very angry at their dog for not responding immediately to the come command. When the dog finally does come after a chase, the owner scolds the dog for not obeying. The dog then begins to associate the come command with an unpleasant result.

It is much easier to avoid bad habits than it is to correct them once they are set. Avoid at all costs giving the come command unless you are sure your Bobtail puppy will come to you. The very young puppy is far more inclined to respond to learning the come command than the older dog that will be less dependent upon you.

Use the command when the puppy is already on his way to you or give the command while walking or running away from the youngster. Clap your hands and sound very happy and excited about having the puppy join in on this game. The very young Bobtail will normally want to stay as close to his owner as possible, especially in strange surroundings. When your puppy sees you moving away, his natural inclination will be to get close to you. This is a perfect time to use the come command.

Later, as a puppy grows more self-confident and independent, you may want to attach a long leash or rope to the puppy's collar to ensure the correct response. Again, do not chase or punish your puppy for not obeying the come command. Doing so in the initial stages of training makes the youngster associate the command with something to fear, resulting in avoidance rather than the immediate positive response you desire. It is imperative that you praise your puppy and give him a treat when he does come to you, even if he voluntarily delays responding for many minutes.

*This owner gives her Old English the hand signal for the stay command—an open palm in front of the dog's face.*

## The Sit and Stay Commands

The sit and stay commands are imperative to your dog's safety. Even very young puppies can learn the sit

*The sit command is the foundation for all the other commands in your Bobtail's training, because it teaches him self-control.*

command quickly, especially if it appears to be a game and a food treat is involved. Your puppy should always be on a leash for his lessons, because a young puppy will walk away when he has decided that you and your lessons are boring.

Give the sit command immediately before lightly pushing down on your puppy's hindquarters to mold him into a sitting position. Praise the puppy lavishly when he does sit, even though it was you that made him sit. Also, giving the puppy a food treat always seems to help get the lesson across more clearly.

Continue holding the dog's rear end down and repeat the sit command several times. If your dog attempts to get up, repeat the command again while exerting pressure on the rear end until the correct position is assumed. Make your Bobtail stay in this position for increasing lengths of time as lessons progress.

If your young student attempts to get up or lie down, he should be corrected by simply saying, "Sit," in a firm voice. This should be accompanied by returning the dog to the desired position. Your dog should only be allowed to get up when you command him to. Do not test young puppy's patience to the limits. Remember that you are dealing with a baby and the attention span of any youngster, canine or human, is relatively short. When you do decide that your puppy can get up, call his name, say "OK," and make a big fuss over him. Praise and a food treat are in order every time your puppy responds correctly.

*The down command is hard for a young, wiggly puppy to get the hang of, but once he masters it, it can be very useful. This pup practices his "down" for the camera.*

Once your puppy has mastered the sitting lesson, you may start on the stay command. With your dog on leash and facing you, command him to sit, then take a step or two backward. If your dog attempts to get up to follow you, firmly say, "Sit, stay." While you are saying this, raise your hand with your palm facing the dog, and again command "Stay."

Any attempt on your dog's part to get up must be corrected at once. Return him to the sit position and repeat, "Stay." Once your Old English Sheepdog begins to understand what you want, you can gradually increase the distance you step back. With a long leash attached to your dog's collar (even a clothesline will do), start with a few steps and gradually increase the distance to several yards. Your Bobtail must eventually learn that the sit/stay command must be obeyed no matter how far away you are. Later on, with advanced training, your dog will learn that the command is to be obeyed even when you move entirely out of sight.

As your Old English Sheepdog masters this lesson and is able to remain in the sit position for as long as you dictate, avoid calling the dog to you. This makes the dog overly anxious to get up and run to you. Instead, walk back to your dog and say "OK," which is a signal that the command is over. Later, when your Bobtail becomes more reliable in this respect, you can call him to you.

The sit/stay lesson can take a considerable amount of time and patience, especially when dealing with a puppy's short attention span. It is best to keep the stay part of the lesson to a minimum until the puppy is at least five or six months old. Everything in a very young Old English Sheepdog's makeup urges him to stay close to you wherever you go. Forcing a very young puppy to operate against his natural instincts can be bewildering for him.

## The Down Command

Once your Bobtail has mastered the sit and stay commands, you may begin working on the down command. Use the down command only when you want the dog to lie down. If you want your dog to get off your sofa or to stop jumping up on people, use the off command. Do not interchange these two commands. Doing so will only serve to confuse your dog and evoking the right response will become nearly impossible.

The down position is especially useful if you want your Bobtail to

*The down command can be used often in everyday life. This Old English Sheepdog lies down on the table for his grooming session.*

*Training will help your Old English Sheepdog become a well-mannered pet that is a joy to be around.*

remain in a particular place for a long period of time. A dog is far more inclined to stay put when he is lying down than when he is sitting. Teaching this command to your Old English Sheepdog may take more time and patience than the previous lessons. It is believed by some animal behaviorists that assuming the down position somehow represents submissiveness to the dog.

With your dog sitting and facing you, hold a treat in your right hand with the excess part of the leash in your left hand. Hold the treat under the dog's nose and slowly bring your hand down to the ground. Your dog will follow the treat with his head and neck. As he does, give the command "down" and exert light pressure on the dog's shoulders with your left hand. If your dog resists the pressure on his shoulders, do not continue pushing down, because this will only create more resistance.

An alternative method of getting your Bobtail into the down position is to move around to the dog's right side and as you draw his attention downward with your right hand, slide your

*Your Old English Sheepdog must be able to heel on a leash if you wish to compete in dog shows.*

left hand or arm under the dog's front legs and gently slide them forward. In the case of a Bobtail puppy, you will undoubtedly have to be on your knees next to the youngster.

As your dog's forelegs begin to slide out to his front, keep moving the treat along the ground until the dog's whole body is lying on the ground, while you continually repeat "down." Once your Bobtail has assumed the position you desire, give him the treat and a lot of praise. Continue assisting your dog into the down position until he does so on his own. Be firm and patient and prepared for those occasional "I have no idea what you mean" looks that your Bobtail student may give you.

## The Heel Command

In learning to heel, your dog will walk on your left side with his shoulder next to your leg, no matter which direction you might go or how quickly you turn. Teaching your Bobtail to heel will not only make your daily walks far more enjoyable, it will make a more tractable companion when the two of you are in crowded or confusing situations.

We have found that a lightweight, chain-link training collar is very useful for the heeling lesson. It provides both quick pressure around the neck and a snapping sound, both of which get the dog's attention. Erroneously referred to as a choke collar, the chain-link collar does not choke the dog if it used properly. After the collar is looped, put it into a letter "P" position and slip it over the dog's head from the front. This will allow the collar to be used properly. Do not leave this collar on your puppy when training sessions are finished, because puppies are ingenious at getting their lower jaw or legs caught in the training chain. Changing to the chain-link collar at training time also signals to your Bobtail that he must get down to the business at hand.

*Praise and rewards are great training motivators for your Old English Sheepdog.*

As you train your puppy to walk along on the leash, you should accustom the youngster to walk on your left side. The leash should cross your body from the dog's collar to your right hand. The excess portion of the leash will be folded into your right hand and your left hand will be used to make corrections with the leash.

A quick short jerk on the leash with your left hand will keep your dog from lunging from side to side, pulling ahead, or lagging back. As you make a correction, give the heel command. Keep the leash slack as long as your dog maintains the proper position at your side.

If your dog begins to drift away, give the leash a sharp jerk, guide the dog back to the correct position, and give the heel command. Do not pull on the lead with steady pressure. A sharp, but gentle jerking motion will get your dog's attention.

## TRAINING CLASSES

There are few limits to what a patient, consistent Bobtail owner can teach his or her dog. For advanced obedience work beyond the basics, it is wise for the Bobtail owner to consider local professional assistance. Professional trainers have had longstanding experience in avoiding the pitfalls of obedience training and can help you to avoid these mistakes.

This training assistance can be obtained in many ways. Classes are particularly good for your Old English Sheepdog's socialization and attentiveness. The dog will learn that he must obey you even when there are other dogs and people around that provide temptation to run off and play. There are free-of-charge classes at many parks and recreation facilities, as well as very formal and sometimes expensive individual lessons with private trainers.

There are also some obedience schools that will take your Bobtail and train him for you. However, unless your schedule doesn't permit you to train your dog, having someone else train the dog for you would be last on our list of recommendations. The rapport that *There are few limits to what a patient, consistent Bobtail owner can teach his or her dog.* develops between the owner who has trained his or her Old English Sheepdog to be a pleasant companion and good canine citizen is very special and well worth the time and patience it requires to achieve such harmony.

## Versatility

The Old English Sheepdog's heritage provides him with the ability to perform in any number of areas. As a herding dog, Old English Sheepdogs can be trained to trialing standards and to compete in various levels of herding trials.

In the right hands, an Old English Sheepdog can be trained to obtain a canine Good Citizen Certificate or to become an Obedience Trial Champion (OTCh). The breed enjoys any number of canine sports, such as agility, Frisbee™, and flyball. Bobtails have successfully been used to bring comfort to the sick and elderly as therapy dogs.

There is actually no boundary to this unique breed's versatility. If the Old English Sheepdog has any limitations at all, they are usually due to human limitations. There can be no doubt that the Old English Sheepdog requires dedication and effort on the part of the owner, but this wonderful breed returns all the work involved tenfold with his affection, jovial spirit, and devotion.

# SPORT of Purebred Dogs

**W**elcome to the exciting and sometimes frustrating sport of dogs. No doubt you are trying to learn more about dogs or you wouldn't be deep into this book. This section covers the basics that may entice you, further your knowledge and help you to understand the dog world.

Dog showing has been a very popular sport for a long time and has been taken quite seriously by some. Others only enjoy it as a hobby.

The Kennel Club in England was formed in 1859, the American Kennel Club was established in 1884 and the Canadian Kennel Club was formed in 1888. The purpose of these clubs was to register purebred dogs and maintain their Stud Books. In the beginning, the concept of registering dogs was not readily accepted. More than 36 million dogs have been enrolled in the AKC Stud Book since its inception in 1888. Presently the

*Successful showing requires dedication and preparation, but most of all, it should be enjoyable for both the dogs and the handlers.*

*Every puppy will benefit from basic training to make him a valued member of the community.* kennel clubs not only register dogs but adopt and enforce rules and regulations governing dog shows, obedience trials and field trials. Over the years they have fostered and encouraged interest in the health and welfare of the purebred dog. They routinely donate funds to veterinary research for study on genetic disorders.

Below are the addresses of the kennel clubs in the United States, Great Britain, and Canada.

The American Kennel Club
260 Madison Avenue
New York, NY 10016
(Their registry is located at: 5580 Centerview Drive, STE 200, Raleigh, NC 27606-3390)

The Kennel Club
1 Clarges Street
Piccadilly, London, WIY 8AB, England

The Canadian Kennel Club
100-89 Skyway Ave.
Etobicoke, Ontario, Canada M9W6R4

Today there are numerous activities that are enjoyable for both the dog and the handler. Some of the activities include conformation showing, obedience competition, tracking, agility, the Canine Good Citizen Certificate, and a wide range of instinct tests that vary from breed to breed. Where you start depends upon your goals which early on may not be readily apparent.

## PUPPY KINDERGARTEN
Every puppy will benefit from this class. PKT is the foundation for all future dog activities from conformation to "couch potatoes." Pet owners should make an effort to attend even if they never expect to show their dog. The class is designed for puppies about three months of age with graduation at approximately five months of age. All the puppies will be in the same age group and, even though some may be a little unruly, there should not be any real problem. This class will teach the puppy some beginning obedience. As in all obedience classes the owner learns how to train his own dog. The PKT class gives the puppy the opportunity to interact with other puppies in the same age group and exposes him to strangers, which is very important. Some dogs grow up with behavior problems, one of them being fear of strangers. As you can see, there can be much to gain from this class.
There are some basic obedience exercises that every dog should learn. Some of these can be started with puppy kindergarten.

## CONFORMATION
Conformation showing is our oldest dog show sport. This type of showing is based on the dog's appearance—that is his structure, movement and attitude. When considering this type of showing, you need to be aware of your breed's standard and

be able to evaluate your dog compared to that standard. The breeder of your puppy or other experienced breeders would be good sources for such an evaluation. Puppies can go through lots of changes over a period of time. Many puppies start out as promising hopefuls and then after maturing may be disappointing as show candidates. Even so this should not deter them from being excellent pets.

Usually conformation training classes are offered by the local kennel or obedience clubs. These are excellent places for training puppies. The puppy should be able to walk on a lead before entering such a class. Proper ring procedure and technique for posing (stacking) the dog will be demonstrated as well as gaiting the dog. Usually certain patterns are used in the ring such as the triangle

*In conformation, your Old English Sheepdog will be judged on how closely he conforms to the standard of the breed.*

or the "L." Conformation class, like the PKT class, will give your youngster the opportunity to socialize with different breeds of dogs and humans too.

It takes some time to learn the routine of conformation showing. Usually one starts at the puppy matches that may be AKC Sanctioned or Fun Matches. These matches are generally for puppies from two or three months to a year old, and there may be classes for the adult over the age of 12 months. Similar to point shows, the classes are divided by sex and after completion of the classes in that breed or variety, the class winners compete for Best of Breed or Variety. The winner goes on to compete in the Group and the Group winners compete for Best in Match. No championship points are awarded for match wins.

A few matches can be great training for puppies even though there is no intention to go on showing. Matches enable the puppy to meet new people and be handled by a stranger—the judge. It is also a change of environment, which broadens the horizon for both dog and handler. Matches and other dog activities boost the confidence of the handler and especially the younger handlers.

Earning an AKC championship is built on a point system, which is different from Great Britain. To become an AKC Champion of Record the dog must earn 15 points. The number of points earned each time depends upon the number of dogs in competition. The number of points available at each show depends upon the breed, its sex and the location of the show. The United States is divided into 12 AKC zones. Each zone has its own set of points. The purpose of the zones is to try to equalize the points available from breed to breed and area to area.The AKC adjusts the point scale annually.

The number of points that can be won at a show are between one and five. Three-, four- and five-point wins are considered majors. Not only does the dog need 15 points won under three different judges, but those points must include two majors under two different judges. Canada also works on a point system but majors are not required.

Dogs always show before bitches. The classes available to those seeking points are: Puppy (which may be divided into 6 to 9 months and 9 to 12 months); 12 to 18 months; Novice; Bred-by-Exhibitor; American-bred; and Open. The class winners of the same sex of each breed or variety compete against each other for Winners Dog and Winners Bitch. A Reserve Winners Dog and Reserve Winners Bitch are also awarded but do not carry any points unless the Winners win is disallowed by AKC. The Winners Dog and Bitch compete with the specials (those dogs that have attained championship) for Best of Breed or Variety, Best of Winners and Best of Opposite Sex. It is possible to pick up an extra point or even a major if the points are higher for the defeated winner than those of Best of Winners. The latter would get the higher total from the defeated winner.

At an all-breed show, each Best of Breed or Variety winner will go on to his respective Group and then the Group winners will compete against each other for Best in Show. There are seven Groups: Sporting, Hounds, Working, Terriers, Toys, Non-Sporting, and Herding. Obviously there are no Groups at speciality shows (those shows that have only one breed or a show such as the American Spaniel Club's Flushing Spaniel Show, which is for all flushing spaniel breeds).

Earning a championship in England is somewhat different since they do not have a point system. Challenge Certificates are awarded if the judge feels the dog is deserving regardless of the number of dogs in competition. A dog must earn three Challenge Certificates under three different judges, with at least one of these Certificates being won after the age of 12 months. Competition is very strong and entries may be higher than they are in the U.S. The Kennel Club's Challenge Certificates are only available at Championship Shows.

*Am. Can. Mex. Ch. Bobmar's Blockbuster ROM, owned by author Marilyn Mayfield.*

In England, The Kennel Club regulations require that certain dogs, Border Collies and

Gundog breeds, qualify in a working capacity (i.e., obedience or field trials) before becoming a full Champion. If they do not qualify in the working aspect, then they are designated a Show Champion, which is equivalent to the AKC's Champion of Record. A Gundog may be granted the title of Field Trial Champion (FT Ch.) if it passes all the tests in the field but would also have to qualify in conformation before becoming a full Champion. A Border Collie that earns the title of Obedience Champion (Ob Ch.) must also qualify in the conformation ring before becoming a Champion.

The US doesn't have a designation full Champion but does award for Dual and Triple Champions. The Dual Champion must be a Champion of Record, and either Champion Tracker, Herding Champion, Obedience Trial Champion or Field Champion. Any dog that has been awarded the titles of Champion of Record, and any two of the following: Champion Tracker, Herding Champion, Obedience Trial Champion or Field Champion, may be designated as a Triple Champion.

The shows in England seem to put more emphasis on breeder judges than those in the US. There is much competition within the breeds. Therefore the quality of the individual breeds should be very good. In the United States we tend to have more "all around judges" (those that judge multiple breeds) and use the breeder judges at the specialty shows. Breeder judges are more familiar with their own breed since they are actively breeding that breed or did so at one time. Americans emphasize Group and Best in Show wins and promote them accordingly.

The shows in England can be very large and extend over several days, with the Groups being scheduled on different days. Though multi-day shows are not common in the US, there are cluster shows, where several different clubs will use the same show site over consecutive days.

Westminster Kennel Club is our most prestigious show although the entry is limited to 2500. In recent years, entry has been limited to Champions. This show is more formal than the majority of the shows with the judges wearing formal attire and the handlers fashionably dressed. In most instances the quality of the dogs is superb. After all, it is a show

*Your Bobtail must be accustomed to extensive grooming if he is to compete in the show ring.*

*The Old English Sheepdog makes a very impressive show dog.*

of Champions. It is a good show to study the AKC registered breeds and is by far the most exciting—especially since it is televised! WKC is one of the few shows in this country that is still benched. This means the dog must be in his benched area during the show hours except when he is being groomed, in the ring, or being exercised.

Typically, the handlers are very particular about their appearances. They are careful not to wear something that will detract from their dog but will perhaps enhance it. American ring procedure is quite formal compared to that of other countries. There is a certain etiquette expected between the judge and exhibitor and among the other exhibitors. Of course it is not always the case but the judge is supposed to be polite, not engaging in small talk or acknowledging how well he knows the handler. There is a more informal and relaxed atmosphere at the shows in other countries. For instance, the dress code is more casual. I can see where this might be more fun for the exhibitor and especially for the novice. The U.S. is very handler-oriented in many of the breeds. It is true, in most instances, that the experienced professional handler can present the dog better and will have a feel for what a judge likes.

*These Bobtails are in position in the show ring. Each handler is responsible for his or her dog's actions in the ring.*

In England, Crufts is The Kennel Club's own show and is most assuredly the largest dog show in the world. They've been known to have an entry of nearly 20,000, and the show lasts four days. Entry is only gained by qualifying through winning in specified classes at another Championship Show. Westminster is strictly conformation, but Crufts exhibitors and spectators enjoy not only conformation but obedience, agility and a multitude of exhibitions as well. Obedience was admitted in 1957 and agility in 1983.

If you are handling your own dog, please give some consideration to your apparel. For sure the dress code at matches is more informal than the point shows. However, you should wear something a little more appropriate than beach attire or ragged jeans and bare feet. If you check out the handlers and see what is presently fashionable, you'll catch on. Men usually dress with a shirt and tie and a nice sports coat. Whether you are male or female, you will want to wear comfortable clothes and shoes. You need to be able to run with your dog and you certainly don't want to take a chance of falling and hurting yourself. Heaven forbid, if nothing else, you'll upset your dog. Women usually wear a dress or two-piece outfit, preferably with pockets to carry bait, comb, brush, etc. In this case men are the lucky ones with all their pockets. Ladies, think about where your dress will be if you need to kneel on the floor and also think about running. Does it allow freedom to do so?

You need to take along a dogcrate, ex pen (if you use one), water pail and water, all required grooming equipment, including hair dryer and extension cord, table, chair for you, bait for dog, and lunch for you and friends. Last but not least, clean up materials, such as plastic bags, paper towels, and perhaps a bath towel and some shampoo—just in case. Don't forget your entry confirmation and directions to the show.

If you are showing in obedience, then you will want to wear pants. Many of our top obedience handlers wear pants that are color-coordinated with their dogs. The philosophy is that imperfections in the black dog will be less obvious next to your black pants.

Whether you are showing in conformation, Junior Showmanship or obedience, you need to watch the clock and be sure you are not late. It is customary to pick up your conformation armband a few minutes before the start of the class. They will not wait for you and if you are on the show grounds and not in the ring, you will upset everyone. It's a little more complicated picking up your obedience armband if you show later in the class. If you have not picked up your armband and they get to your number, you may not be allowed to show. It's best to pick up your armband early, but then you may show earlier than expected if other handlers don't pick up. Customarily all conflicts should be discussed with the judge prior to the start of the class.

## Junior Showmanship

The Junior Showmanship Class is a wonderful way to build self-confidence even if there are no aspirations of staying with the dog-show game later in life. Frequently, Junior Showmanship becomes the background of those who become successful exhibitors/handlers in the future. In some instances it is taken very seriously, and success is measured in terms of wins. The Junior Handler is judged solely on his ability and skill in presenting his dog. The dog's conformation is not to be considered by the judge. Even so the condition and grooming of the dog may be a reflection upon the handler.

Usually the matches and point shows include different classes. The Junior Handler's dog may be entered in a breed or obedience class and even shown by another person in that class. Junior Showmanship classes are usually divided by age and perhaps sex. The age is determined by the handler's age on the day of the show.

*Your Old English Sheepdog can also compete for the Canine Good Citizen Certificate, which is designed to encourage owners to properly train their dogs.*

### CANINE GOOD CITIZEN

The AKC sponsors a program to encourage dog owners to train their dogs. Local clubs perform the pass/fail tests, and dogs who pass are awarded a Canine Good Citizen Certificate. Proof of vaccination is required at the time of participation. The test includes:

1. Accepting a friendly stranger.
2. Sitting politely for petting.
3. Appearance and grooming.
4. Walking on a loose leash.
5. Walking through a crowd.
6. Sit and down on command/staying in place.
7. Come when called.
8. Reaction to another dog.
9. Reactions to distractions.
10. Supervised separation.

If more effort was made by pet owners to accomplish these exercises, fewer dogs would be cast off to the humane shelter.

## OBEDIENCE

Obedience is necessary, without a doubt, but it can also become a wonderful hobby or even an obsession. Obedience classes and competition can provide wonderful companionship, not only with your dog but with your classmates or fellow competitors. It is always gratifying to discuss your dog's problems with others who have had similar experiences. The AKC acknowledged Obedience around 1936, and it has changed tremendously even though many of the exercises are basically the same. Today, obedience competition is just that—very competitive. Even so, it is possible for every obedience exhibitor to come home a winner (by earning qualifying scores) even though he/she may not earn a placement in the class.

*The versatile Old English Sheepdog can compete in many different events, including obedience and herding trials.*

Most of the obedience titles are awarded after earning three qualifying scores (legs) in the appropriate class under three different judges. These classes offer a perfect score of 200, which is extremely rare. Each of the class exercises has its own point value. A leg is earned after receiving a score of at least 170 and at least 50 percent of the points available in each exercise. The titles are:

After achieving the UD title, you may feel inclined to go after the UDX and/or OTCh. The UDX (Utility Dog Excellent) title went into effect in January 1994. It is not easily attained. The title requires qualifying simultaneously ten times in Open B and Utility B but not necessarily at consecutive shows.

The OTCh (Obedience Trial Champion) is awarded after the dog has earned his UD and then goes on to earn 100 championship points, a first place in Utility, a first place in Open and another first place in either class. The placements must be won under three different judges at all-breed obedience trials. The points are determined by the number of dogs competing in the Open B and Utility B classes. The OTCh title precedes the dog's name.

Obedience matches (AKC Sanctioned, Fun, and Show and Go) are usually available. Usually they are sponsored by the local obedience clubs. When preparing an obedience dog

for a title, you will find matches very helpful. Fun Matches and Show and Go Matches are more lenient in allowing you to make corrections in the ring. This type of training is usually very necessary for the Open and Utility Classes. AKC Sanctioned Obedience Matches do not allow corrections in the ring since they must abide by the AKC Obedience Regulations. If you are interested in showing in obedience, then you should contact the AKC for a copy of the Obedience Regulations.

## TRACKING

Tracking is officially classified obedience. There are three tracking titles available: Tracking Dog (TD), Tracking Dog Excellent (TDX), Variable Surface Tracking (VST). If all three tracking titles are obtained, then the dog officially becomes a CT

*Even if you never enter a show, the attention and training you give your Bobtail will only benefit the both of you in the long run.*

*The Old English Sheepdog is an intelligent and agile dog that is eager to please his master and easily trained.*

(Champion Tracker). The CT will go in front of the dog's name.

A TD may be earned anytime and does not have to follow the other obedience titles. There are many exhibitors that prefer tracking to obedience, and there are others who do both.

## AGILITY

Agility was first introduced by John Varley in England at the Crufts Dog Show, February 1978, but Peter Meanwell, competitor and judge, actually developed the idea. It was officially recognized in the early '80s. Agility is extremely popular in England and Canada and growing in popularity in the US. The AKC acknowledged agility in August 1994. Dogs must be at least 12 months of age to be entered. It is a fascinating sport that the dog, handler and spectators enjoy to the utmost. Agility is a spectator sport! The dog performs off lead. The handler either runs with his dog or positions himself on the course and directs his dog with verbal and hand signals over a timed course over or through a variety of obstacles including a time out or pause. One of the main drawbacks to agility is finding a place to train. The obstacles take up a lot of space and it is very time consuming to put up and take down courses.

*Herding competitions are a great place for your Bobtail to show off his considerable skills and to be recognized for his special talents.*

The titles earned at AKC agility trials are Novice Agility Dog (NAD), Open Agility Dog (OAD), Agility Dog Excellent (ADX), and Master Agility Excellent (MAX). In order to acquire an agility title, a dog must earn a qualifying score in its respective class on three separate occasions under two different judges. The MAX will be awarded after earning ten qualifying scores in the Agility Excellent Class.

## PERFORMANCE TESTS

During the last decade the American Kennel Club has promoted performance tests—those events that test the different breeds' natural abilities. This type of event encourages a handler to devote even more time to his dog and retain the natural instincts of his breed heritage. It is an important part of the wonderful world of dogs.

## Herding Titles

For all Herding breeds and Rottweilers and Samoyeds.

Entrants must be at least nine months of age and dogs with limited registration (ILP) are eligible. The Herding program is divided into Testing and Trial sections. The goal is to demonstrate proficiency in

*Obedience training allows the Old English Sheepdog and his owner to develop a close bond formed through working together.*

herding livestock in diverse situations. The titles offered are Herding Started (HS), Herding Intermediate (HI), and Herding Excellent (HX). Upon completion of the HX a Herding Championship may be earned after accumulating 15 championship points.

*The above information has been taken from the AKC Guidelines for the appropriate events.*

## GENERAL INFORMATION

Obedience, tracking and agility allow the purebred dog with an Indefinite Listing Privilege (ILP) number or a limited registration to be exhibited and earn titles. Application must be made to the AKC for an ILP number.

The American Kennel Club publishes a monthly *Events* magazine that is part of the *Gazette*, their official journal for the sport of purebred dogs. The *Events* section lists upcoming shows and the secretary or superintendent for them. The majority of the conformation shows in the US are overseen by licensed superintendents. Generally the entry closing date is approximately two-and-a-half weeks before the actual show. Point shows are fairly expensive, while the match shows cost about one third of the point show entry fee. Match shows usually take entries the day of the show but some are pre-entry. The best way to find match show information is through your local kennel club. Upon asking, the AKC can provide you with a list of superintendents, and you can write and ask to be put on their mailing lists.

Obedience trial and tracking test information is available through the AKC. Frequently these events are not superintended, but put on by the host club. Therefore you would make the entry with the event's secretary.

As you have read, there are numerous activities you can share with your dog. Regardless what you do, it does take teamwork. Your dog can only benefit from your attention and training. We hope this chapter has enlightened you and hope, if nothing else, you will attend a show here and there. Perhaps you will start with a puppy kindergarten class, and who knows where it may lead!

*Training to compete is not an easy task, but the satisfaction you'll receive when you accomplish your goals will be rewarding for both you and your dog.*

# Health Care

Veterinary medicine has become far more sophisticated than what was available to our ancestors. This can be attributed to the increase in household pets and consequently the demand for better care for them. Also human medicine has become far more complex. Today diagnostic testing in veterinary medicine parallels human diagnostics. Because of better technology we can expect our pets to live healthier lives thereby increasing their life spans.

## The First Checkup

You will want to take your new puppy/dog in for its first checkup within 24 to 72 hours after acquiring it. Many breeders strongly recommend this check up and so do the humane shelters. A puppy/dog can appear healthy but it may have a serious problem that is not apparent to the layman. Most pets have some type of a minor flaw that may never cause a real problem.

Unfortunately if he/she should have a serious problem, you will want to consider the consequences of keeping the pet and the attachments that will be formed, which may be broken prematurely. Keep in mind there are many healthy dogs looking for good homes.

This first checkup is a good time to establish yourself with the veterinarian and learn the office policy regarding their hours and how they handle emergencies. Usually the breeder or another conscientious pet owner is a good reference for locating a capable veterinarian. You should be aware that not all veterinarians give the same quality of service. Please do not make your selection on the least expensive clinic, as they may be short changing your pet. There is the possibility that eventually it will cost you more due to improper diagnosis, treatment, etc. If you are selecting a new veterinarian, feel free to ask for a tour of the clinic. You should inquire about making an appointment for a tour since all clinics are working clinics, and therefore may not be available all day for sightseers. You may worry less if you see where your pet will be spending the day if he ever needs to be hospitalized.

## The Physical Exam

Your veterinarian will check your pet's overall condition, which includes listening to the heart; checking the respiration; feeling the abdomen, muscles and joints; checking the mouth, which includes the gum color and signs of gum disease along with plaque buildup; checking the ears for signs of an infection or ear mites; examining the eyes; and, last but not least, checking the condition of the skin and coat.

He should ask you questions regarding your pet's eating and elimination habits and invite you to relay your questions. It is a good idea to prepare a list so as not to forget anything. He should discuss the proper diet and the quantity to be fed. If this should differ from your breeder's recommendation, then you should convey to him the breeder's choice and see if he approves. If he recommends changing the diet, then this should be done over a few days so as not to cause a gastrointestinal upset. It is customary to take in a fresh stool sample (just a small amount) for a test for intestinal parasites. It must be fresh, preferably within 12 hours, since the eggs hatch quickly and after hatching will not be observed under the microscope. If your pet isn't obliging then, usually the technician can take one in the clinic.

*Maternal antibodies protect puppies from disease for the first few weeks of life. Because these antibodies are only temporarily effective, vaccinations are necessary.*

## Immunizations

It is important that you take your puppy/dog's vaccination record with you on your first visit. In case of a puppy, presumably the breeder has seen to the vaccinations up to the time you acquired custody. Veterinarians differ in their vaccination protocol. It is not unusual for your puppy to have received vaccinations for distemper, hepatitis, leptospirosis, parvovirus and parainfluenza every two to three weeks from the age of five or six weeks. Usually this is a combined injection and is typically called the DHLPP. The DHLPP is given through at least 12 to 14 weeks of age, and it is customary to continue with another parvovirus vaccine at 16 to 18 weeks. You may wonder why so many immunizations are necessary. No one knows for sure when the puppy's maternal antibodies are gone, although it is customarily accepted that distemper antibodies are gone by 12 weeks. Usually parvovirus antibodies are gone by 16 to 18 weeks of age. However, it is possible for the maternal antibodies to be gone at a much earlier age or even a later age. Therefore immunizations are started at an early age. The vaccine will not give immunity as long as there are maternal antibodies.

The rabies vaccination is given at three or six months of age depending on your local laws. A vaccine for bordetella (kennel cough) is advisable and can be given anytime from the age of five weeks. The coronavirus is not commonly given unless there is a problem locally. The Lyme vaccine is necessary in endemic areas. Lyme disease has been reported in 47 states.

## Distemper

This is virtually an incurable disease. If the dog recovers, he is subject to severe nervous disorders. The virus attacks every tissue in the body and resembles a bad cold with a fever. It can

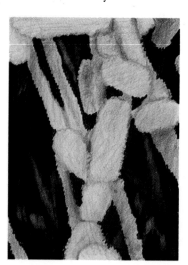

cause a runny nose and eyes and cause gastrointestinal disorders, including a poor appetite, vomiting and diarrhea. The virus is carried by raccoons, foxes, wolves, mink and other dogs. Unvaccinated youngsters and senior citizens are very susceptible. This is still a common disease.

*Bordetella attached to canine cilia. Otherwise known as kennel cough, this disease is highly contagious and should be vaccinated against routinely.*

## Hepatitis

This is a virus that is most serious in very young dogs. It is spread by contact with an infected animal or its stool or urine. The virus affects the liver and kidneys and is characterized by high fever, depression and lack of appetite. Recovered animals may be afflicted with chronic illnesses.

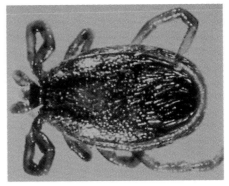

*The deer tick is the most common carrier of Lyme disease. Photo courtesy of Virbac Laboratories, Inc., Fort Worth, Texas.*

## Leptospirosis

This is a bacterial disease transmitted by contact with the urine of an infected dog, rat or other wildlife. It produces severe symptoms of fever, depression, jaundice and internal bleeding and was fatal before the vaccine was developed. Recovered dogs can be carriers, and the disease can be transmitted from dogs to humans.

## Parvovirus

This was first noted in the late 1970s and is still a fatal disease. However, with proper vaccinations, early diagnosis and prompt treatment, it is a manageable disease. It attacks the bone marrow and intestinal tract. The symptoms include depression, loss of appetite, vomiting, diarrhea and collapse. Immediate medical attention is of the essence.

## Rabies

This is shed in the saliva and is carried by raccoons, skunks, foxes, other dogs and cats. It attacks nerve tissue, resulting in paralysis and death. Rabies can be transmitted to people and is virtually always fatal. This disease is reappearing in the suburbs.

## Bordetella (Kennel Cough)

The symptoms are coughing, sneezing, hacking and retching accompanied by nasal discharge usually lasting from a few days to several weeks. There are several disease-producing organisms responsible for this disease. The present vaccines are helpful but do not protect for all the strains. It usually is not life threatening but in some instances it can progress to a serious bronchopneumonia. The disease is highly contagious. The vaccination should be given routinely for dogs that come in contact with other dogs, such as through boarding, training class or visits to the groomer.

## Coronavirus

This is usually self limiting and not life threatening. It was first noted in the late '70s about a year before parvovirus. The virus produces a yellow/brown stool and there may be depression, vomiting and diarrhea.

## Lyme Disease

This was first diagnosed in the United States in 1976 in Lyme, CT in people who lived in close proximity to the deer tick. Symptoms may include acute lameness, fever, swelling of joints and loss of appetite. Your veterinarian can advise you if you live in an endemic area.

*Your Old English Sheepdog should receive all his necessary immunizations early in life to ensure a healthy first year.*

*Regular annual veterinarian visits are important to your Bobtail's lifelong health maintenance and to prevent potential problems.*

After your puppy has completed his puppy vaccinations, you will continue to booster the DHLPP once a year. It is customary to booster the rabies one year after the first vaccine and then, depending on where you live, it should be boostered every year or every three years. This depends on your local laws. The Lyme and corona vaccines are boostered annually and it is recommended that the bordetella be boostered every six to eight months.

## ANNUAL VISIT

I would like to impress the importance of the annual check up, which would include the booster vaccinations, check for intestinal parasites and test for heartworm. Today in our very busy world it is rush, rush and see "how much you can get for how little." Unbelievably, some non-veterinary businesses have entered into the vaccination business. More harm than good can come to your dog through improper vaccinations, possibly from inferior vaccines and/or the wrong schedule. More than likely you truly care about your companion dog and over the years you have devoted much time and expense to his well being. Perhaps you are unaware that a vaccination is not just a vaccination. There is more involved. Please, please follow through with regular physical examinations. It is so important for your veterinarian to know your dog and this is especially true during middle age through the geriatric years. More than likely your older dog will require more than one physical a year. The annual physical is good preventive medicine. Through early diagnosis and subsequent treatment your dog can maintain a longer and better quality of life.

## INTESTINAL PARASITES

### Hookworms

These are almost microscopic intestinal worms that can cause anemia and therefore serious problems, including death, in young puppies. Hookworms can be transmitted to humans through penetration of the skin. Puppies may be born with them.

### Roundworms

These are spaghetti-like worms that can cause a potbellied appearance and dull coat along with more severe symptoms, such as vomiting, diarrhea and coughing. Puppies acquire these while in the mother's uterus and through lactation. Both hookworms and roundworms may be acquired through ingestion.

### Whipworms

These have a three-month life cycle and are not acquired through the dam. They cause intermittent diarrhea usually with

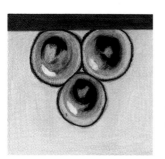

mucus. Whipworms are possibly the most difficult worm to eradicate. Their eggs are very resistant to most environmental factors and can last for years until the proper conditions enable them

*Roundworms eggs, as seen on a fecal evaluation. The eggs must develop for at least 12 days before they are infective.*

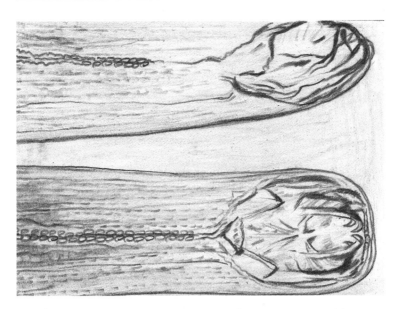

*Hookworms are almost microscopic intestinal worms that can cause anemia and therefore serious problems, even death.* to mature. Whipworms are seldom seen in the stool.

Intestinal parasites are more prevalent in some areas than others. Climate, soil and contamination are big factors contributing to the incidence of intestinal parasites. Eggs are passed in the stool, lay on the ground and then become infective in a certain number of days. Each of the above worms has a different life cycle. Your best chance of becoming and remaining worm-free is to always pooper-scoop your yard. A fenced-in yard keeps stray dogs out, which is certainly helpful.

I would recommend having a fecal examination on your dog twice a year or more often if there is a problem. If your dog has a positive fecal sample, then he will be given the appropriate medication and you will be asked to bring back another stool sample in a certain period of time (depending on the type of worm) and then be rewormed. This process goes on until he has at least two negative samples. The different types of worms require different medications. You will be wasting your money and doing your dog an injustice by buying over-the-counter medication without first consulting your veterinarian.

## OTHER INTERNAL PARASITES

### Coccidiosis and Giardiasis
These protozoal infections usually affect puppies, especially in places where large numbers of puppies are brought together. Older dogs may harbor these infections but do not show signs unless they are stressed. Symptoms include diarrhea, weight loss and lack of appetite. These infections are not always apparent in the fecal examination.

### Tapeworms
Seldom apparent on fecal floatation, they are diagnosed frequently as rice-like segments around the dog's anus and the base of the tail. Tapeworms are long, flat and ribbon like, sometimes several feet in length, and made up of many segments about five-eighths of an inch long. The two most common types of tapeworms found in the dog are:
(1)  First the larval form of the flea tapeworm parasite must mature in an intermediate host, the flea, before it can become infective. Your dog acquires this by ingesting the flea through licking and chewing.
(2)  Rabbits, rodents and certain large game animals serve as intermediate hosts for other species of tapeworms. If your dog should eat one of these infected hosts, then he can acquire tapeworms.

## HEARTWORM DISEASE
This is a worm that resides in the heart and adjacent blood vessels of the lung that produces microfilaria, which circulate in the bloodstream. It is possible for a dog to be infected with any number of worms from one to a hundred that can be 6 to 14 inches long. It is a life-threatening disease, expensive to treat and easily prevented. Depending on where you live, your veterinarian may recommend a preventive year-round and either an annual or semiannual blood test. The most common preventive is given once a month.

## EXTERNAL PARASITES

### Fleas
These pests are not only the dog's worst enemy but also

enemy to the owner's pocketbook. Preventing is less expensive than treating, but regardless we'd prefer to spend our money elsewhere. Likely, the majority of our dogs are allergic to the bite of a flea, and in many cases it only takes one flea bite. The protein in the flea's saliva is the culprit. Allergic dogs have a reaction, which usually results in a "hot spot." More than likely such a reaction will involve a trip to the veterinarian for treatment. Yes, prevention is less expensive. Fortunately today there are several good products available.

If there is a flea infestation, no one product is going to correct the problem. Not only will the dog require treatment so will the environment. In general flea collars are not very effective although there is now available an "egg" collar that will kill the eggs on the dog. Dips are the most economical but they are messy. There are some effective shampoos and treatments available through pet shops and veterinarians. An oral tablet arrived on the American market in 1995 and was popular in Europe the previous year. It sterilizes the female flea but will not kill adult fleas. Therefore the tablet, which is given monthly, will decrease the flea population but is not a "cure-all." Those dogs that suffer from flea-bite allergy will still be subjected to the bite of the flea. Another popular parasiticide is permethrin, which is applied to the back of the dog in one or two places depending on the dog's weight. This product works as a

*The more time your Bobtail spends outside, the better chance he has of picking up parasites like fleas and ticks.*

*If your dog is scratching excessively, it could be an indication of a parasite infestation. Be sure to check your dog's coat thoroughly if he shows any signs of irritation.*

repellent causing the flea to get "hot feet" and jump off. Do not confuse this product with some of the organophosphates that are also applied to the dog's back.

Some products are not usable on young puppies. Treating fleas should be done under your veterinarian's guidance. Frequently it is necessary to combine products and the layman does not have the knowledge regarding possible toxicities. It is hard to believe but there are a few dogs that do have a natural resistance to fleas. Nevertheless it would be wise to treat all pets at the same time. Don't forget your cats. Cats just love to prowl the neighborhood and consequently return with unwanted guests.

Adult fleas live on the dog but their eggs drop off the dog into the environment. There they go through four larval stages before reaching adulthood, and thereby are able to jump back on the poor unsuspecting dog. The cycle resumes and takes between 21 to 28 days under ideal conditions. There are environmental products available that will kill both the adult fleas and the larvae.

## Ticks

Ticks carry Rocky Mountain Spotted Fever, Lyme disease and can cause tick paralysis. They should be removed with tweezers, trying to pull out the head. The jaws carry disease. There is a tick preventive collar that does an excellent job. The ticks automatically back out on those dogs wearing collars.

*The cat flea is the most common flea of both cats and dogs. Courtesy of Fleabusters, Rx for Fleas, Inc., Fort Lauderdale, Florida.*

## Sarcoptic Mange

This is a mite that is difficult to find on skin scrapings. The pinnal reflex is a good indicator of this disease. Rub the ends of the pinna (ear) together and the dog will start scratching with his foot. Sarcoptes are highly contagious to other dogs and to humans although they do not live long on humans. They cause intense itching.

## Demodectic Mange

This is a mite that is passed from the dam to her puppies. It affects youngsters age three to ten months. Diagnosis is confirmed by skin scraping. Small areas of alopecia around the eyes, lips and/or forelegs become visible. There is little itching unless there is a secondary bacterial infection. Some breeds are afflicted more than others.

## Cheyletiella

This causes intense itching and is diagnosed by skin scraping. It lives in the outer layers of the skin of dogs, cats, rabbits and humans. Yellow-gray scales may be found on the back and the rump, top of the head and the nose.

## TO BREED OR NOT TO BREED

More than likely your breeder has requested that you have your puppy neutered or spayed. Your breeder's request is based on what is healthiest for your dog and what is most beneficial for your breed. Experienced and conscientious breeders devote many years into developing a bloodline. In order to do this, he makes every effort to plan each breeding in regard to conformation, temperament and health. This type of breeder does his best to perform the necessary testing (i.e., OFA, CERF, testing for inherited blood disorders, thyroid, etc.). Testing is expensive and sometimes very disheartening when a favorite dog doesn't pass his health tests. The health history pertains not only to the breeding stock but to the immediate ancestors. Reputable breeders do not want their offspring to be bred

*Spaying or neutering your Bobtail will help prevent certain diseases, as well as help control the pet population.*

indiscriminately. Therefore you may be asked to neuter or spay your puppy. Of course there is always the exception, and your breeder may agree to let you breed your dog under his direct supervision. This is an important concept. More and more effort is being made to breed healthier dogs.

## Spay/Neuter

There are numerous benefits of performing this surgery at six months of age. Unspayed females are subject to mammary and ovarian cancer. In order to prevent mammary cancer she must be spayed prior to her first heat cycle. Later in life, an unspayed female may develop a pyometra (an infected uterus), which is definitely life threatening.

*The Old English Sheepdog is generally a healthy breed, and if loved and well cared for, will live a long and productive life.*

Spaying is performed under a general anesthetic and is easy on the young dog. As you might expect it is a little harder on the older dog, but that is no reason to deny her the surgery. The surgery removes the ovaries and uterus. It is important to remove all the ovarian tissue. If some is left behind, she could remain attractive to males. In order to view the ovaries, a reasonably long incision is necessary. An ovariohysterectomy is considered major surgery.

Neutering the male at a young age will inhibit some characteristic male behavior that owners frown upon. Some boys will not hike their legs and mark territory if they are neutered at six months of age. Also neutering at a young age has hormonal benefits, lessening the chance of hormonal aggressiveness.

Surgery involves removing the testicles but leaving the scrotum. If there should be a retained testicle, then he definitely needs to be neutered before the age of two or three years. Retained testicles can develop into cancer. Unneutered males are at risk for testicular cancer, perineal fistulas, perianal tumors and fistulas and prostatic disease.

Intact males and females are prone to housebreaking accidents. Females urinate frequently before, during and after heat cycles, and males tend to mark territory if there is a female in heat. Males may show the same behavior if there is a visiting dog or guests.

Surgery involves a sterile operating procedure equivalent to human surgery. The incision site is shaved, surgically scrubbed and draped. The veterinarian wears a sterile surgical gown, cap, mask and gloves. Anesthesia should be monitored by a registered technician. It is customary for the veterinarian to recommend a pre-anesthetic blood screening, looking for metabolic problems and a ECG rhythm strip to check for normal heart function. Today anesthetics are equal to human anesthetics, which enables your dog to walk out of the clinic the same day as surgery.

Some folks worry about their dog gaining weight after being neutered or spayed. This is usually not the case. It is true that some dogs may be less active so they could develop a problem, but most dogs are just as active as they were before surgery. However, if your dog should begin to gain, then you need to decrease his food and see to it that he gets a little more exercise.

## Medical Problems

### Anal Sacs

These are small sacs on either side of the rectum that can cause the dog discomfort when they are full. They should empty when the dog has a bowel movement. Symptoms of inflammation or impaction are excessive licking under the tail and/or a bloody or sticky discharge from the anal area. Some breeders recommend emptying the sacs on a regular schedule when bathing the dog. Many veterinarians prefer this isn't done unless there are symptoms. You can express the sacs by squeezing the two sacs (at the five and seven o'clock positions) in and up toward the anus. Take precautions not to get in the way of the foul-smelling fluid that is expressed. Some dogs object to this procedure so it would be wise to have someone hold the head. Scooting is caused by anal-sac irritation and not worms.

## Colitis

The stool may be frank blood or blood tinged and is the result of inflammation of the colon. Colitis, sometimes intermittent, can be the result of stress, undiagnosed whipworms, or perhaps idiopathic (no explainable reason). If intermittent bloody stools are an ongoing problem, you should probably feed a diet higher in fiber. Seek professional help if your dog feels poorly and/or the condition persists.

## Conjunctivitis

Many breeds are prone to this problem. The conjunctiva is the pink tissue that lines the inner surface of the eyeball except the clear, transparent cornea. Irritating substances such as bacteria, foreign matter or chemicals can cause it to become reddened and swollen. It is important to keep any hair trimmed from around the eyes. Long hair stays damp and aggravates the problem. Keep the eyes cleaned with warm water and wipe away any matter that has accumulated in the corner of the eyes. If the condition persists, you should see your veterinarian. This problem goes hand in hand with keratoconjunctivitis sicca.

*Make sure that your Old English Sheepdog's eyes are clear and free from redness or irritation.*

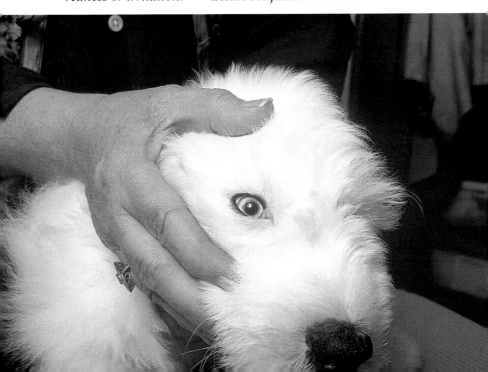

# DENTAL CARE for Your Dog's Life

So you've got a new puppy! You also have a new set of puppy teeth in your household. Anyone who has ever raised a puppy is abundantly aware of these new teeth. Your puppy will chew anything it can reach, chase your shoelaces, and play "tear the rag" with any piece of clothing it can find. When puppies are newly born, they have no teeth. At about four weeks of age, puppies of most breeds begin to develop their deciduous or baby teeth. They begin eating semi-solid food, fighting and biting with their litter mates, and learning discipline from their mother. As their new teeth come in, they inflict more pain on their mother's breasts, so her feeding sessions become less frequent and shorter. By six or eight weeks, the mother will start growling to warn her pups when they are fighting too roughly or hurting her as they nurse too much with their new teeth.

*Cleaning your Old English Sheepdog's teeth should be a part of your regular grooming routine.*

Puppies need to chew. It is a necessary part of their physical and mental development. They develop muscles and necessary life skills as they drag objects around, fight over possession, and vocalize alerts and warnings. Puppies chew on things to explore their world. They are using their sense of taste to determine what is food and what is not. How else can they tell an electrical cord from a lizard? At about four months of age, most puppies begin shedding their baby teeth. Often these teeth need some help to come out and make way for the permanent teeth. The incisors (front teeth) will be replaced first. Then, the adult canine or fang teeth erupt. When the baby tooth is not shed before the permanent tooth comes in, veterinarians call it a retained deciduous tooth. This condition will often cause gum infections by trapping hair and debris between the permanent tooth and the retained baby tooth. Nylafloss® is an excellent device for puppies to use. They can toss it, drag it, and chew on the many surfaces it presents. The baby teeth can catch in the nylon material, aiding in their removal. Puppies that have adequate chew toys will have less destructive behavior, develop more

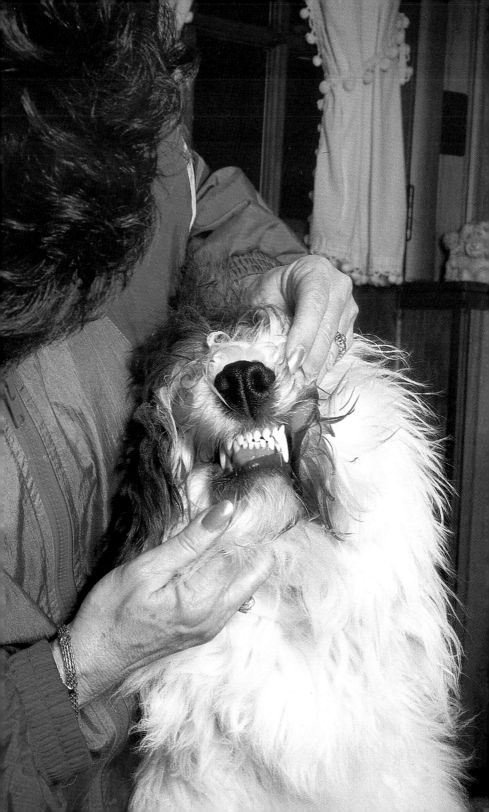

*A thorough oral exam is an important part of your Old English Sheepdog's annual veterinary checkup.*

physically, and have less chance of retained deciduous teeth.

During the first year, your dog should be seen by your veterinarian at regular intervals. Your veterinarian will let you know when to bring in your puppy for vaccinations and parasite examinations. At each visit, your veterinarian should inspect the lips, teeth, and mouth as part of a complete physical examination. You should take some part in the maintenance of your dog's oral health. You should examine your dog's mouth weekly throughout his first year to make sure there are no sores, foreign objects, tooth problems, etc. If your dog drools excessively, shakes its head, or has bad breath, consult your veterinarian. By the time your dog is six months old, the permanent teeth are all in and plaque can start to accumulate on the tooth surfaces. This is when your dog needs to develop good dental-care habits to prevent calculus build-up on its teeth. Brushing is best. That is a fact that cannot be denied. However, some dogs do not like their teeth brushed regularly, or you may not be able to accomplish the task. In that case, you should consider a product that will help prevent plaque and calculus build-up.

*If you train your dog to having good chewing habits while he is a puppy, he will have healthier teeth throughout his life.*

The Plaque Attackers® and Galileo Bone® are other excellent choices for the first three years of a dog's life. Their shapes make them interesting for the dog. As the dog chews on them, the solid polyurethane massages the gums which improves the blood circulation to the periodontal tissues. Projections on the chew devices increase the surface and are in contact with the tooth for more efficient cleaning. The unique shape and consistency prevent your dog from exerting excessive force on his own teeth or from breaking off pieces of the bone. If your dog is an aggressive chewer or weighs more than 55 pounds (25 kg), you should consider giving him a Nylabone®, the most durable chew product on the market.

The Gumabones ®, made by the Nylabone Company, is constructed of strong polyurethane, which is softer than nylon. Less powerful chewers prefer the Gumabones® to the Nylabones®. A super option for your dog is the Hercules Bone®, a uniquely shaped bone named after the great Olympian for its exception strength. Like all Nylabone products, they are specially scented to make them attractive to your dog. Ask your veterinarian about these bones and he will validate the good doctor's prescription: Nylabones® not only give your dog a good chewing workout but also help to save your dog's teeth (and even his life, as it protects him from possible fatal periodontal diseases).

By the time dogs are four years old, 75% of them have periodontal disease. It is the most common infection in dogs. Yearly examinations by your veterinarian are essential to maintaining your dog's good health. If your veterinarian detects periodontal disease, he or she may recommend a prophylactic cleaning. To do a thorough cleaning, it will be necessary to put your dog under anesthesia. With modern gas anesthetics and monitoring equipment, the procedure is pretty safe. Your veterinarian will scale the teeth with an ultrasound scaler or hand instrument. This removes the calculus from the teeth. If there are calculus deposits below the gum line, the veterinarian will plane the roots to make them smooth. After all of the calculus has been removed, the teeth are polished with pumice in a polishing cup. If any medical or surgical treatment is needed, it is done at this time. The final step would be fluoride treatment and your follow-up treatment at home. If the periodontal disease is advanced, the veterinarian may prescribe a medicated mouth rinse or antibiotics for use at home. Make sure your dog has safe, clean and attractive chew toys and treats. Chooz® treats are another way of using a consumable treat to help keep your dog's teeth clean.

Rawhide is the most popular of all materials for a dog to chew. This has never been good news to dog owners, because rawhide is inherently very dangerous for dogs. Thousands of dogs have died from rawhide, having swallowed the hide after it has become soft and mushy, only to cause stomach and intestinal blockage. A new rawhide product on the market has finally solved the problem of rawhide: molded Roar-Hide® from Nylabone. These are composed of processed, cut up, and melted American rawhide injected into your dog's favorite shape: a dog bone. These dog-safe devices smell and taste like rawhide but don't break up. The ridges on the bones help to fight tartar build-up on the teeth and they last ten times longer than the usual rawhide chews.

As your dog ages, professional examination and cleaning should become more frequent. The mouth should be inspected at least once a year. Your veterinarian may recommend visits every six months. In the geriatric patient, organs such as the heart, liver, and kidneys do not function as well as when they were young. Your veterinarian will probably want to test these organs' functions prior to using general anesthesia for dental cleaning. If your dog is a good chewer and you work closely with your veterinarian, your dog can keep all of its teeth all of its life. However, as your dog ages, his sense of smell, sight, and taste will diminish. He may not have the desire to chase, trap or chew his toys. He will also not have the energy to chew for long periods, as arthritis and periodontal disease make chewing painful. This will leave you with more responsibility for keeping his teeth clean and healthy. The dog that would not let you brush his teeth at one year of age, may let you brush his teeth now that he is ten years old.

*Toys are excellent tools to relieve your dog's need to chew and keep his teeth and jaw occupied.*

If you train your dog with good chewing habits as a puppy, he will have healthier teeth throughout his life.

# TRAVELING with Your Dog

The earlier you start traveling with your new puppy or dog, the better. He needs to become accustomed to traveling. However, some dogs are nervous riders and become carsick easily. It is helpful if he starts with an empty stomach. Do not despair, as it will go better if you continue taking him with you on short fun rides. How would you feel if every time you rode in the car you stopped at the doctor's for an injection? You would soon dread that nasty car. Older dogs that tend to get carsick may have more of a problem adjusting to traveling. Those dogs that are having a serious problem may benefit from some medication prescribed by the veterinarian.

*You'll never have to leave your Old English Sheepdog behind if you accustom him to traveling at an early age.*

Do give your dog a chance to relieve himself before getting into the car. It is a good idea to be prepared for a clean up with a leash, paper towels, bag and terry cloth towel.

The safest place for your dog is in a fiberglass crate, although close confinement can promote carsickness in some dogs. If your dog is nervous you can try letting him ride on the seat next to you or in someone's lap.

An alternative to the crate would be to use a car harness made for dogs and/or a safety strap attached to the harness or collar. Whatever you do, do not let your dog ride in the back of a pickup truck unless he is securely tied on a very short lead. I've seen trucks stop quickly and, even though the dog was tied, it fell out and was dragged.

Another advantage of the crate is that it is a safe place to leave him if you need to run into the store. Otherwise you wouldn't be able to leave the windows down. Keep in mind that while many dogs are overly protective in their crates, this may not be enough to deter dognappers. In some states it is against the law to leave a dog in the car unattended.

Never leave a dog loose in the car wearing a collar and leash. More than one dog has killed himself by hanging. Do

not let him put his head out an open window. Foreign debris can be blown into his eyes. When leaving your dog unattended in a car, consider the temperature. It can take less than five minutes to reach temperatures over 100 degrees Fahrenheit.

## TRIPS

Perhaps you are taking a trip. Give consideration to what is best for your dog–traveling with you or boarding. When traveling by car, van or motor home, you need to think ahead about locking your vehicle. In all probability you have many valuables in the car and do not wish to leave it unlocked. Perhaps most valuable and not replaceable is your dog. Give thought to securing your vehicle and providing adequate ventilation for him. Another consideration for you when traveling with your dog is medical problems that may arise and little inconveniences, such as exposure to external parasites. Some areas of the country are quite flea infested. You may want to carry flea spray with you. This is even a good idea when staying in motels. Quite possibly you are not the only occupant of the room.

*If your dog is to compete in dog shows, he must get used to extensive travel.*

*Crates are the safest way for your Bobtails to travel in the car.*    Unbelievably many motels and even hotels do allow canine guests, even some very first-class ones. Gaines Pet Foods Corporation publishes *Touring With Towser*, a directory of domestic hotels and motels that accommodate guests with dogs. Their address is Gaines TWT, PO Box 5700, Kankakee, IL, 60902. Call ahead to any motel that you may be considering and see if they accept pets. Sometimes it is necessary to pay a deposit against room damage. The management may feel reassured if you mention that your dog will be crated. If you do travel with your dog, take along plenty of baggies so that you can clean up after him. When we all do our share in cleaning up, we make it possible for motels to continue accepting our pets. As a matter of fact, you should practice cleaning up everywhere you take your dog.

Depending on where your are traveling, you may need an up-to-date health certificate issued by your veterinarian. It is good policy to take along your dog's medical information, which would include the name, address and phone number of your veterinarian, vaccination record, rabies certificate, and any medication he is taking.

## AIR TRAVEL

When traveling by air, you need to contact the airlines to check their policy. Usually you have to make arrangements up to a couple of weeks in advance for traveling with your dog. The airlines require your dog to travel in an airline approved fiberglass crate. Usually these can be purchased through the airlines but they are also readily available in most pet-supply stores. If your dog is not accustomed to a crate, then it is a good idea to get him acclimated to it before your trip. The day of the actual trip you should withhold water about one hour ahead of departure and no food for about 12 hours. The airlines generally have temperature restrictions, which do not allow pets to travel if it is either too cold or too hot. Frequently these restrictions are based on the temperatures at the

*The Old English Sheepdog is such an easygoing and accommodating breed that you can take him almost anywhere.*

departure and arrival airports. It's best to inquire about a health certificate. These usually need to be issued within ten days of departure. You should arrange for non-stop, direct flights and if a commuter plane should be involved, check to see if it will carry dogs. Some don't. The Humane Society of the United States has put together a tip sheet for airline traveling. You can receive a copy by sending a self-addressed stamped envelope to:

The Humane Society of the United States
Tip Sheet
2100 L Street NW
Washington, DC 20037.

Regulations differ for traveling outside of the country and

*Make sure you allow your Bobtail plenty of time outside to eliminate and exercise when he accompanies you when you travel.*

are sometimes changed without notice. Well in advance you need to write or call the appropriate consulate or agricultural department for instructions. Some countries have lengthy quarantines (six months), and countries differ in their rabies vaccination requirements. For instance, it may have to be given at least 30 days ahead of your departure.

Do make sure your dog is wearing proper identification including your name, phone number and city. You never know when you might be in an accident and separated from your dog. Or your dog could be frightened and somehow manage to escape and run away.

Another suggestion would be to carry in-case-of-emergency instructions. These would include the address and phone number of a relative or friend, your veterinarian's name, address and phone number, and your dog's medical information.

BOARDING KENNELS

Perhaps you have decided that you need to board your dog. Your veterinarian can recommend a good boarding facility or possibly a pet sitter that will come to your house. It is customary for the boarding kennel to ask for proof of vaccination for the DHLPP, rabies and bordetella vaccine. The bordetella should have been given within six months of boarding. This is for your protection. If they do not ask for this proof I would not board at their kennel. Ask about flea control. Those dogs that suffer flea-bite allergy can get in trouble at a boarding kennel. Unfortunately boarding kennels are limited on how much they are able to do.

For more information on pet sitting, contact NAPPS:
National Association of Professional Pet Sitters
1200 G Street, NW
Suite 760
Washington, DC 20005.

Some pet clinics have technicians that pet sit and technicians that board clinic patients in their homes. This may be an alternative for you. Ask your veterinarian if they have an employee that can help you. There is a definite advantage of having a technician care for your dog, especially if your dog is on medication or is a senior citizen.

*A well-trained and well-socialized Old English Sheepdog makes a suitable traveling companion.*

You can write for a copy of *Traveling With Your Pet* from ASPCA, Education Department, 441 E. 92nd Street, New York, NY 10128.

# IDENTIFICATION and Finding the Lost Dog

There are several ways of identifying your dog. The old standby is a collar with dog license, rabies, and ID tags. Unfortunately collars have a way of being separated from the dog and tags fall off. We're not suggesting you shouldn't use a collar and tags. If they stay intact and on the dog, they are the quickest way of identification.

For several years owners have been tattooing their dogs. Some tattoos use a number with a registry. Here lies the problem because there are several registries to check. If you wish to tattoo, use your social security number. The humane shelters have the means to trace it. It is usually done on the inside of the rear thigh. The area is first shaved and numbed. There is no pain, although a few dogs do not

*Old English Sheepdogs possess plenty of curiosity and energy. Make sure that your dog is closely supervised when outside so that he doesn't become lost or separated from you.*

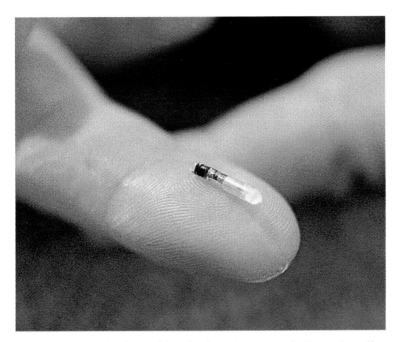

*The newest method of identification is the microchip, a computer chip no bigger than a grain of rice that can help you track your dog's whereabouts.*

like the buzzing sound. Occasionally tattooing is not legible and needs to be redone.

The newest method of identification is microchipping. The microchip is a computer chip that is no larger than a grain of rice. The veterinarian implants it by injection between the shoulder blades. The dog feels no discomfort. If your dog is lost and picked up by the humane society, they can trace you by scanning the microchip, which has its own code. Microchip scanners are friendly to other brands of microchips and their registries. The microchip comes with a dog tag saying the dog is microchipped. It is the safest way of identifying your dog. I personally recommend the microchip.

## FINDING THE LOST DOG

I am sure you will agree that there would be little worse than losing your dog. Responsible pet owners rarely lose their dogs. They do not let their dogs run free because they don't want harm to come to them. Not only that but in most, if not all, states there is a leash law.

Beware of fenced-in yards. They can be a hazard. Dogs find ways to escape either over or under the fence. Another fast exit is through the gate that perhaps the neighbor's child left unlocked.

Below is a list that hopefully will be of help to you if you need it. Remember don't give up, keep looking. Your dog is worth your efforts.

1. Contact your neighbors and put flyers with a photo on it in their mailboxes. Information you should include would be the dog's name, breed, sex, color, age, source of identification, when your dog was last seen

*Make sure you have a clear recent picture of your dog available to distribute in case he becomes lost.*

and where, and your name and phone numbers. It may be helpful to say the dog needs medical care. Offer a *reward*.

2. Check all local shelters daily. It is also possible for your dog to be picked up away from home and end up in an out-of-the-way shelter. Check these too. Go in person. It is not good enough to call. Most shelters are limited on the time they can hold dogs then they are put up for adoption or euthanized. There is the possibility that your dog will not make it to the shelter for several days. Your dog could have been wandering or someone may have tried to keep him.

3. Notify all local veterinarians. Call and send flyers.

4. Call your breeder. Frequently breeders are contacted when one of their breed is found.

5. Contact the rescue group for your breed.

6. Contact local schools—children may have seen your dog.

7. Post flyers at the schools, groceries, gas stations, convenience stores, veterinary clinics, groomers and any other place that will allow them.

8. Advertise in the newspaper.

9. Advertise on the radio.

# BEHAVIOR and Canine Communication

S tudies of the human/animal bond point out the importance of the unique relationships that exist between people and their pets. Those of us who share our lives with pets understand the special part they play through companionship, service and protection. For many, the pet/owner bond goes beyond simple companionship; pets are often considered members of the family. A leading pet food manufacturer recently conducted a nationwide survey of pet owners to gauge just how important pets were in their lives. Here's what they found:

*The bond between humans and animals, especially loving dogs like the Bobtail, is a strong one.*

- 76 percent allow their pets to sleep on their beds
- 78 percent think of their pets as their children
- 84 percent display photos of their pets, mostly in their homes
- 84 percent think that their pets react to their own emotions
- 100 percent talk to their pets
- 97 percent think that their pets understand what they're saying

Are you surprised?

Senior citizens show more concern for their own eating habits when they have the responsibility of feeding a dog. Seeing that their dog is routinely exercised encourages the owner to think of schedules that otherwise may seem unimportant to the senior citizen. The older owner may be arthritic and feeling poorly but with responsibility for his dog he has a reason to get up and get moving. It is a big plus if his dog is an attention seeker who will demand such from his owner.

Over the last couple of decades, it has been shown that pets relieve the stress of those who lead busy lives. Owning a pet has been known to lessen the occurrence of heart attack and stroke.

Many single folks thrive on the companionship of a dog. Lifestyles are very different from a long time ago, and today

more individuals seek the single life. However, they receive fulfillment from owning a dog.

Most likely the majority of our dogs live in family environments. The companionship they provide is well worth the effort involved. In my opinion, every child should have the opportunity to have a family dog. Dogs teach responsibility through understanding their care, feelings and even respecting their life cycles. Frequently those children who have not been exposed to dogs grow up afraid of dogs, which isn't good. Dogs sense timidity and some will take advantage of the situation.

Today more dogs are serving as service dogs. Since the origination of the Seeing Eye dogs years ago, we now have trained hearing dogs. Also dogs are trained to provide service for the handicapped and are able to perform many different tasks for their owners. Search and Rescue dogs, with their handlers, are sent throughout the world to assist in recovery of disaster victims. They are life savers.

Therapy dogs are very popular with nursing homes, and some

*Many people feel that owning a dog enriches their lives and reduces stress. Who could help but smile at an adorable Bobtail puppy?*

*Bobtails that have been socialized with other dogs from an early age will have no trouble getting along with others.* hospitals even allow them to visit. The inhabitants truly look forward to their visits. They wanted and were allowed to have visiting dogs in their beds to hold and love.

Nationally there is a Pet Awareness Week to educate students and others about the value and basic care of our pets. Many countries take an even greater interest in their pets than Americans do. In those countries the pets are allowed to accompany their owners into restaurants and shops, etc. In the US this freedom is only available to our service dogs. Even so we think very highly of the human/animal bond.

## CANINE BEHAVIOR

Canine behavior problems are the number-one reason for pet owners to dispose of their dogs, either through new homes, humane shelters or euthanasia. Unfortunately there are too many owners who are unwilling to devote the necessary time to properly train their dogs. On the other hand, there are those who not only are concerned about inherited health problems but are also aware of the dog's mental stability.

You may realize that a breed and his group relatives (i.e., sporting, hounds, etc.) show tendencies to behavioral characteristics. An experienced breeder can acquaint you with his breed's personality. Unfortunately many breeds are labeled with poor temperaments when actually the breed as a whole is not affected but only a small percentage of individuals within the breed.

*Watching littermates play with each other can tell you a lot about a dog's personality. These adorable pups compete for "top dog."*

Inheritance and environment contribute to the dog's behavior. Some naïve people suggest inbreeding as the cause of bad temperaments. Inbreeding only results in poor behavior if the ancestors carry the trait. If there are excellent temperaments behind the dogs, then inbreeding will promote good temperaments in the offspring. Did you ever consider that inbreeding is what sets the characteristics of a breed? A purebred dog is the end result of inbreeding. This does not spare the mixed-breed dog from the same problems. Mixed-breed dogs frequently are the offspring of purebred dogs.

Not too many decades ago most of our dogs led a different lifestyle than what is prevalent today. Usually mom stayed home so the dog had human companionship and someone to discipline it if needed. Not much was expected from the dog. Today's mom works and everyone's life is at a much faster pace.

The dog may have to adjust to being a "weekend" dog. The family is gone all day during the week, and the dog is left to his own devices for entertainment. Some dogs sleep all day waiting for their family to come home and others become wigwam wreckers if given the opportunity. Crates do ensure

*By breeding only the best-quality dogs, good temperament and soundness is passed down from generation to generation.*

the safety of the dog and the house. However, he could become a physically and emotionally cripple if he doesn't get enough exercise and attention. We still appreciate and want the companionship of our dogs although we expect more from them. In many cases we tend to forget dogs are just that—*dogs* not human beings.

## SOCIALIZING AND TRAINING

Many prospective puppy buyers lack experience regarding the proper socialization and training needed to develop the type of pet we all desire. In the first 18 months, training does take some work. It is easier to start proper training before there is a problem that needs to be corrected.

The initial work begins with the breeder. The breeder should start socializing the puppy at five to six weeks of age and cannot let up. Human socializing is critical up through 12 weeks of age and likewise important during the following months. The litter should be left together during the first few weeks but it is necessary to separate them by ten weeks of age. Leaving them together after that time will increase competition for litter dominance. If puppies are not socialized with people by 12 weeks of age, they will be timid in later life.

The eight- to ten-week age period is a fearful time for puppies. They need to be handled very gently around children and adults. There

*A loving and playful relationship with his dam and littermates is the first step to a well-socialized puppy.*

*The good-natured and fun-loving Old English Sheepdog is usually up for any kind of family activity. This Bobtail is tired out after trick-or-treating.*

should be no harsh discipline during this time. Starting at 14 weeks of age, the puppy begins the juvenile period, which ends when he reaches sexual maturity around six to 14 months of age. During the juvenile period he needs to be introduced to strangers (adults, children and other dogs) on the home property. At sexual maturity he will begin to bark at strangers and become more protective. Males start to lift their legs to urinate but if you desire you can inhibit this behavior by walking your boy on leash away from trees, shrubs, fences, etc.

Perhaps you are thinking about an older puppy. You need to inquire about the puppy's social experience. If he has lived in a kennel, he may have a hard time adjusting to people and environmental stimuli. Assuming he has had a good social upbringing, there are advantages to an older puppy.

Training includes puppy kindergarten and a minimum of one to two basic training classes. During these classes you will learn how to dominate your youngster. This is especially important if you own a large breed of dog. It is somewhat

*Training is very important to produce a well-mannered pet, especially in a large-sized breed like the Old English Sheepdog.*

harder, if not nearly impossible, for some owners to be the Alpha figure when their dog towers over them. You will be taught how to properly restrain your dog. This concept is important. Again it puts you in the Alpha position. All dogs need to be restrained many times during their lives. Believe it or not, some of our worst offenders are the eight-week-old puppies that are brought to our clinic. They need to be gently restrained for a nail trim but the way they carry on you would think we were killing them. In comparison, their vaccination is a "piece of cake." When we ask dogs to do something that is not agreeable to them, then their worst comes out. Life will be easier for your dog if you expose him at a young age to the necessities of life—proper behavior and restraint.

## Understanding the Dog's Language

Most authorities agree that the dog is a descendent of the wolf. The dog and wolf have similar traits. For instance both are pack oriented and prefer not to be isolated for long periods of time. Another characteristic is that the dog, like the wolf, looks to the leader—Alpha—for direction. Both the wolf and the dog communicate through body language, not only within their pack but with outsiders.

Every pack has an Alpha figure. The dog looks to you, or should look to you, to be that leader. If your dog doesn't receive the proper training and guidance, he very well may replace you as Alpha. This would be a serious problem and is certainly a disservice to your dog.

*Don't let that cute, innocent face fool you! Like all puppies, Bobtails are perfectly willing and able to get into all types of mischief.*

Eye contact is one way the Alpha wolf keeps order within his pack. You are Alpha so you must establish eye contact with your puppy. Obviously your puppy will have to look at you. Practice eye contact even if you need to hold his head for five to ten seconds at a time. You can give him a treat as a reward. Make sure your eye contact is gentle and not threatening. Later, if he has been naughty, it is permissible to give him a long, penetrating look. There are some older dogs that never learned eye contact as puppies and cannot accept eye contact. You should avoid eye contact with these dogs since they feel threatened and will retaliate as such.

## Body Language

The play bow, when the forequarters are down and the hindquarters are elevated, is an invitation to play. Puppies play fight, which helps them learn the acceptable limits of biting. This is necessary for later in their lives. Nevertheless, an owner may be falsely reassured by the playful nature of his dog's aggression. Playful aggression toward another dog or human

may be an indication of serious aggression in the future.
Owners should never play fight or play tug-of-war with any dog
that is inclined to be dominant.
Signs of submission are:
    1.  Avoids eye contact.
    2.  Active submission—the dog crouches down, ears back
    and the tail is lowered.
    3.  Passive submission—the dog rolls on his side with his
    hindlegs in the air and frequently urinates.
Signs of dominance are:
    1.  Makes eye contact.
    2.  Stands with ears up, tail up and
    the hair raised on his neck.
    3.  Shows dominance over another
    dog by standing at right angles over
    it.
Dominant dogs tend to behave in
    characteristic ways such as:
    1.  The dog may be unwilling to

*Your Bobtails may try to assert their independence, but they must always know that you are the leader in your relationship.*

*The more people and animals your dog meets, the better socialized he will become. This Bobtail and his Cocker Spaniel friend seem to be getting along just fine.*

move from his place (i.e., reluctant to give up the sofa if the owner wants to sit there).

2. He may not part with toys or objects in his mouth and may show possessiveness with his food bowl.

3. He may not respond quickly to commands.

4. He may be disagreeable for grooming and dislikes to be petted.

Dogs are popular because of their sociable nature. Those that have contact with humans during the first 12 weeks of life regard them as a member of their own species–their pack. All dogs have the potential for both dominant and submissive behavior. Only through experience and training do they learn to whom it is appropriate to show which behavior. Not all dogs are concerned with dominance but owners need to be aware of that potential. It is wise for the owner to establish his dominance early on.

A human can express dominance or submission toward a dog in the following ways:

1. Meeting the dog's gaze signals dominance. Averting the gaze signals submission. If the dog growls or threatens,

averting the gaze is the first avoiding action to take—it may prevent attack. It is important to establish eye contact in the puppy. The older dog that has not been exposed to eye contact may see it as a threat and will not be willing to submit.

2. Being taller than the dog signals dominance; being lower signals submission. This is why, when attempting to make friends with a strange dog or catch the runaway, one should kneel down to his level. Some owners see their dogs become dominant when allowed on the furniture or on the bed. Then he is at the owner's level.

3. An owner can gain dominance by ignoring all the dog's social initiatives. The owner pays attention to the dog only when he obeys a command.

No dog should be allowed to achieve dominant status over any adult or child. Ways of preventing are as follows:

1. Handle the puppy gently, especially during the three- to four-month period.

2. Let the children and adults handfeed him and teach him to take food without lunging or grabbing.

3. Do not allow him to chase children or joggers.

4. Do not allow him to jump on people or mount their legs. Even females may be inclined to mount. It is not only a male habit.

5. Do not allow him to growl for any reason.

6. Don't participate in wrestling or tug-of-war games.

7. Don't physically punish puppies for aggressive behavior. Restrain him from repeating the infraction and teach an alternative behavior. Dogs should earn everything they receive from their owners. This would include sitting to receive petting or treats, sitting before going out the door and sitting to receive the collar and leash. These types of exercises reinforce the owner's dominance.

*Your Old English Sheepdog puppy may display fear at certain times. Respect his feelings and give him a chance to become used to the situation.*

Young children should never be left alone with a dog. It is important that children learn some basic obedience commands so they have some control over the dog. They will gain the respect of their dog.

## FEAR

One of the most common problems dogs experience is being fearful. Some dogs are more afraid than others. On the lesser side, which is sometimes humorous to watch, dogs can be afraid of a strange object. They act silly when something is out of place in the house. We call his problem perceptive intelligence. He realizes the abnormal within his known environment. He does not react the same way in strange environments since he does not know what is normal.

On the more serious side is a fear of people. This can result in backing off, seeking his own space and saying "leave me alone" or it can result in an aggressive behavior that may lead to challenging the person. Respect that the dog wants to be left alone and give him time to come forward. If you approach the cornered dog, he may resort to snapping. If you leave him alone, he may decide to come forward, which should be rewarded with a treat.

Some dogs may initially be too fearful to take treats. In these cases it is helpful to make sure the dog hasn't eaten for about 24 hours. Being a little hungry encourages him to accept the treats, especially if they are of the "gourmet" variety.

Dogs can be afraid of numerous things, including loud noises and thunderstorms. Invariably the owner rewards (by comforting) the dog when it

*Puppies have an innate curiosity and an eagerness to explore. Proper supervision and discipline will help your Bobtail to avoid getting into trouble.*

*Even the most adorable puppies can develop behavior problems, which is why it is important to be a firm and fair owner.*

shows signs of fearfulness. When your dog is frightened, direct his attention to something else and act happy. Don't dwell on his fright.

## AGGRESSION

Some different types of aggression are: predatory, defensive, dominance, possessive, protective, fear induced, noise provoked, "rage" syndrome (unprovoked aggression), maternal and aggression directed toward other dogs. Aggression is the most common behavioral problem encountered. Protective breeds are expected to be more aggressive than others but with the proper upbringing they can make very dependable companions. You need to be able to read your dog.

Many factors contribute to aggression including genetics and environment. An improper environment, which may include the living conditions, lack of social life, excessive punishment, being attacked or frightened by an aggressive dog, etc., can all influence a dog's behavior. Even spoiling him and giving too much praise may be detrimental. Isolation and the lack of human contact or exposure to frequent teasing by children or adults also can ruin a good dog.

Lack of direction, fear, or confusion lead to aggression in those dogs that are so inclined. Any obedience exercise, even the sit and down, can direct the dog and overcome fear and/or confusion. Every dog should learn these commands as a youngster, and there should be periodic reinforcement.

When a dog is showing signs of aggression, you should speak calmly (no screaming or hysterics) and firmly give a command that he understands, such as the sit. As soon as your dog obeys, you have assumed your dominant position. Aggression presents a problem because there may be danger to others. Sometimes it is an emotional issue. Owners may consciously or unconsciously encourage their dog's aggression. Other owners show responsibility by accepting the problem and taking measures to keep it under control. The owner is responsible for his dog's actions, and it is not wise to take a chance on someone being bitten, especially a child. Euthanasia is the solution for some owners and in severe cases this may be the best choice. However, few dogs are that dangerous and very few are that much of a threat to their owners. If caution is exercised and professional help is gained early on, most cases can be controlled.

Some authorities recommend feeding a lower protein (less than 20 percent) diet. They believe this can aid in reducing aggression. If the dog loses weight, then vegetable oil can be added. Veterinarians and behaviorists are having some success with pharmacology. In many cases treatment is possible and can improve the situation.

If you have done everything according to "the book" regarding training and socializing and are still having a behavior problem, don't procrastinate. It is important that the problem gets attention before it is out of hand. It is estimated that 20 percent of a veterinarian's time may be devoted to dealing with problems before they become so intolerable that the dog is separated from its home and owner. If your veterinarian isn't able to help, he should refer you to a behaviorist.

# SUGGESTED READING

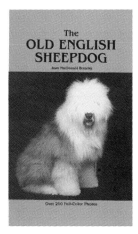

PS817
*The Old English Sheepdog*
*256 pages, over 120 full-color photos*

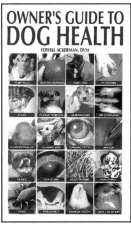

TS-249
*Owner's Guide to Dog Health*
*224 pages, over 190 full-color photos*

JG117
*A New Owner's Guide to Dog Training*
*160 pages, over 140 full-color photos*

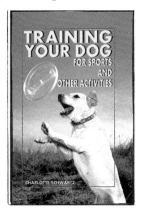

TS-258
*Training Your Dog for Sports and Other Activities*
*160 pages, over 200 full-color photos.*

# INDEX

Adolescence, 50
—feeding, 50
Aggression, 157
Agility, 86, 103
American Kennel
 Club, 13, 88, 89, 104
Anal sacs, 122
Bathing, 58, 66
Bloat, 50
Body language, 151
Boarding kennels, 137
Bordetella, 111
Breeders, 30
British Isles, 11
Brushing, 60
Canadian Kennel
 Club, 90
Canine Good Citizen,
 86, 99
Chewing, 124
Cheyletiella, 119
Clipping, 62
Coccidiosis, 116
Colitis, 123
Come, 77
Conformation, 90
Conjunctivitis, 123
Coronavirus, 112
Crates, 70, 130
—travel, 130
Diet sheet, 44
Diet, 54
—special, 58
Distemper, 43, 110
Dog food, 54
Dominance, 152
Down, 82
Ear care, 63
Exercise, 67
Fear, 156
Feeding, 52
Fezziwig Black Eyed
 Susan, 16
Fezziwig Ceiling Zero,
 16
Fiennes, Alice and
 Richard, 6

Fleas, 116
Flyball, 86
Giardiasis, 116
Grooming, 58
—brushing, 60
—clipping, 62
—equipment, 60
Health concerns, 33,
 122
Health guarantee, 44
Health record, 43
Heartworm, 116
Heel, 84
Hepatitis, 43, 111
Herding, 11, 86, 104
—titles, 104
—trials, 86
Hip dysplasia, 34, 56
Hookworms, 114
Housebreaking, 70
Humane Society of the
 United States, 134
Immunizations, 35,
 109
Junior showmanship,
 98
Juvenile cataracts, 34
Kennel Club, The, 90
Kennel cough, 111
Leash training, 75
Leptospirosis, 43, 111
Lloyd, Freeman, 15
Lyme disease, 112,
 119
Mange, 119
Microchipping, 139
Morgan, J. Pierpont,
 15
Nail trimming, 65
*Natural History of
 Dogs, The*, 6
Neutering, 39, 120
No, 75
Obedience, 100
Old English Sheepdog
 Club of America, 16,
 32

Orthopedic
 Foundation for
 Animals (OFA), 35
Parasites, 114, 116
—external, 116
—internal, 114
Parvovirus, 43, 111
Pedigree, 43
Performance tests,104
Periodontal disease,
 128
Pet sitters, 137
Puppy kindergarten,
 90
Rabies, 111
Registration
 certificate, 43
Roundworms, 114
Sit, 79
Socialization, 46, 67,
 148
Spaying, 39, 120
Stay, 79
Submission, 152
Supplementation, 56
Tapeworms, 116
Tattooing, 138
Temperament, 46
Therapy dog, 86
Ticks, 119
Tracking, 102
Training, 74, 148
—basic, 74
—classes, 85
—crate, 70
Van Rensselaer,
 Hendrik and Serena,
 16
Veterinarian, 108
—annual visit, 113
—first checkup, 108
—physical exam, 109
Wade, William, 14
Westminster Kennel
 Club, 15
Whipworms, 114